Global Perspectives
on Social Issues

Global Perspectives on Social Issues

Pornography

Richard Procida and Rita J. Simon

LEXINGTON BOOKS
Lanham • Boulder • New York • Oxford

LEXINGTON BOOKS

Published in the United States of America
by Lexington Books
A Member of the Rowman & Littlefield Publishing Group
4720 Boston Way, Lanham, Maryland 20706
www.rowmanlittlefield.com

PO Box 317
Oxford
OX2 9RU, UK

British Library Cataloguing in Publication Information Available

Library of Congress Cataloging-in-Publication Data

Procida, Richard, 1964-
    Global perspectives on social issues : pornography / Richard Procida and
    Rita J. Simon
        p. cm.
    Includes index.   ℐ
    ISBN 0-7391-0501-9
    1. Pornography. 2. Pornography—Government policy. 3. Pornography—Social
aspects. I. Simon, Rita James. II. Title.
    HQ471 .P763 2003
    363.4'7—dc21   2002012175

Printed in the United States of America

To the memory of
Ismael "E.C." Sanchez Jr. (October 22, 1963–March 14, 1985),
Lisa Ann Shaw (September 5, 1963–March 14, 1985),
and those who passed in the same accident
—RP

To the memory of
my husband, Julian Lincoln Simon,
a strong believer in freedom
—RJS

Contents

Introduction   ix

1 The United States, Canada, and Australia   1

2 Western Europe and Eastern Europe   35

3 Asia   65

4 Other Nations   89

Conclusion   97

Appendix: Comparative Regulation of Child Pornography
on the Internet
   Sherry Mitchell   103

Index   125

About the Authors   135

Introduction

Global Perspectives on Social Issues: Pornography surveys laws, regulations, and public opinion regarding pornography in a sample of countries around the world. We represent different regions of the world so as to identify the ways different cultures understand and cope with this phenomenon. In so doing, we address the following issues: (1) Is censorship of pornography correlated with authoritarianism? (2) Is censorship of pornography a "slippery slope" leading to the censorship of other, more valuable speech, such as political and artistic speech? (3) Is pornography a causal factor in violence against women and the sexual abuse of children? and (4) Is the United States more, or less, prudish than other nations around the world, particularly other western democratic nations? These issues address many of the arguments made by anti-censorship and anti-pornography advocates around the world.

Detailed information is provided for the United States, Canada, and Australia, and selected and representative countries in Western and Eastern Europe and Asia. Brief information is reported for selected countries in Central and South America, the Middle East, and Africa.

The concluding chapter summarizes the materials presented earlier and makes recommendations about the statutes, policies, and strategies societies should adopt vis-à-vis the availability and distribution of pornographic materials.

The appendix focuses on child pornography from a comparative perspective.

Chapter One

The United States, Canada, and Australia

The United States is the pornography capital of the world. Americans produce and consume more pornography than any other nation. Although nudity is entirely absent from broadcast television, U.S. laws are extremely protective of the material. Just across the border, in Canada, pornography is available, but degrading and violent pornography is subject to obscenity prosecution.

The concept of obscenity originated in England, but the United States abandoned the English definition in 1957 and has since created an approach that has been followed by other nations throughout the world, including Israel, the Philippines, and Canada. Canada, however, has gone one step further in adopting the American-born civil rights approach while utilizing a variant of the American "community standards" approach. Canadian policy, however, is more in line with European policy in that Canada is less tolerant of violent media than is the United States. One may suspect that Canada also seeks to protect its culture from ubiquitous American influence.

We begin our survey with the United States because the United States is the world's greatest producer of entertainment, including adult entertainment. Its laws could serve as a baseline to compare the approaches of other nations to how Americans perceive themselves and their approach to pornography. Is the U.S. approach the best? Is it the only way? Are we more enlightened? More free? More prudish? Or more fair? These are some of the questions we hope to answer with this survey. Most of all, we hope this survey will educate both sides of the debate toward a better understanding of one another and the ways different nations cope with pornography.

UNITED STATES

By far the leading international exporter of pornographic films, America produces more than 150 new titles a week and spends more than 8 billion dollars a year on hard-core videos, peep shows, live sex acts, adult cable programming, computer porn, and sex magazines. This is reportedly more than Hollywood's domestic box-office receipts and larger than all the annual revenues generated by rock and country music recordings combined.[1] Americans rented more than 410 million adult videos in 1991, and 2,400 new adult videos were produced and distributed in 1993.[2] Adult bookstores dot the American landscape. The most often read sexually explicit magazine is *Playboy*. As many as one in ten women, and one in five men, read the magazine.[3] While subject to local zoning ordinances and state entrance-age restrictions, the stores are otherwise generally ignored by local law enforcement,[4] and the last state censor's office closed in 1981.[5] The American characteristic of staunch individualism, coupled with constitutional protection of speech and the press, works against government regulation of pornography.

Legal Approaches

The First Amendment to the Constitution of the United States stipulates that "Congress shall make no law . . . abridging the freedom of speech, or of the press, or the right of the people peaceably to assemble, and to petition the Government for a redress of grievances."[6] The Fourteenth Amendment made the Constitution applicable to the state governments,[7] meaning that the right will be upheld against state legislatures as well as the federal government.[8]

In *Roth v. United States*, the U.S. Supreme Court held that obscenity is not constitutionally protected speech under the First Amendment.[9] In so doing, it abandoned the British *Hicklin* test and developed its own definition for obscenity. The *Hicklin* test defined obscenity as material that has a tendency to deprave and corrupt those who are likely to view the material.[10] The *Roth* Court introduced the "appeal-to-the-prurient-interest" requirement.[11] The Court defined material appealing to the prurient interest as "material having a tendency to excite lustful thoughts,"[12] and defined prurient as "[i]tching; longing; uneasy with desire or longing; of persons, having itching, morbid or lascivious longings; of desire, curiosity, or propensity, lewd."[13] Material was obscene "if, considered as a whole, its predominant appeal is to the prurient interest, i.e., a shameful or morbid interest in nudity, sex, or excretion, and if it goes substantially beyond customary limits of candor in the description or representation of such matters."[14] Though all erotic material has a propensity to excite lustful thoughts, not all erotic material is obscene. What is required is that the interest have a shameful or morbid quality to it.[15]

Following *Roth*, the U.S. Supreme Court issued rulings that dramatically changed how the country dealt with erotic literature. These rulings involved works like *Lady Chatterley's Lover*, *Tropic of Cancer*, and *Fanny Hill*. Before 1966 these books could not legally be published in the United States, but afterward writings that had literary merit were no longer to be considered obscene even if they contained sexually explicit material. The Court declared five categories of speech to be essentially outside the reach of the First Amendment: speech that is likely to incite imminent lawless action; defamation; obscenity; fighting words; and child pornography.[16] In so doing, the *Roth* Court applied some form of the "clear and present danger test." This test strictly limits the government's reach to cases where a direct and immediate threat to the public is imminent. Indirect or remote harm is insufficient to warrant restrictions on speech. These decisions culminated in the 1973 decision of *Miller v. California*.[17]

Miller v. California articulated the current test for determining whether given material is obscene. The tryer of fact must determine the following:

> (a) whether "the average person, applying contemporary community standards" would find the work, taken as a whole, appeals to the prurient interest; (b) whether the work depicts or describes, in a

patently offensive way, sexual conduct specifically defined by the applicable state law; and (c) whether the work, taken as a whole, lacks serious literary, artistic, political, or scientific value.[18]

In effect, the *Miller* test limits obscenity to hard-core pornography which depicts normal or perverted ultimate sexual acts, acts of masturbation and excretory functions, and the lewd exhibition of the genitals that violates both state laws and local community standards.[19] Community standards, however, vary widely. What is considered "obscene" in Kansas may be considered fine art in New York. Community standards can also change. What seemed quite shocking several years ago may look tame by today's standards, just as today's "pornography" may barely raise an eyebrow tomorrow.[20]

Recent attempts to define pornography as a civil rights violation have failed in the United States. Prominent feminists, such as Catherine MacKinnon and Andrea Dworkin, passed legislation in Indianapolis defining pornography as a form of hate propaganda that threatens women's safety and promotes discrimination.[21] The United States Seventh Circuit Court of Appeals rejected this approach, finding it to be "viewpoint discrimination" forbidden by the Constitution.[22] In other words, the Seventh Circuit Court of Appeals held the ordinance unconstitutional because it was discrimination based on the content of speech.

The court's interpretation of the First Amendment led it to disregard the potential effects of pornography. According to the Seventh Circuit's decision, the more severe the effect, the more the material should be protected. The fact that the material has an effect on the opinions and actions of others is evidence that it is speech protected by the First Amendment. The First Amendment requires that we allow even the most vile expressions. After all, if we are to allow Nazis freedom of speech, we must also allow pornographers the same rights, especially if we disagree with their message.

The Supreme Court, however, has allowed an outright ban on child pornography, citing the harm to the children involved.[23] Intervening to protect children from harm, the Supreme Court, in *New York v. Ferber*,[24] upheld a New York law prohibiting the distribution of child pornography. The Court found the use of children in the production of pornography to be injurious to the child's "physiological, emotional, and mental health" and "intrinsically related to the sexual abuse of children."[25] It could therefore be banned in order to eliminate the economic incentive for its production.

In fact, many of the restrictions on pornography are designed to protect children from exposure to sexually explicit material. Television stations show almost no explicit nudity, and both television and radio limit adult content to late evening hours.[26] The voluntary movie rating system focuses on preventing minors from viewing sexually explicit materials. The Supreme Court has allowed local communities to use zoning laws to restrict the dissemination of sexually explicit materials.[27] Adult bookstores and movie theaters are not allowed near schools. When it comes to violent media, however, the United States is much more liberal. For example, when the state of Missouri sought to restrict the sale or rental of violent videotapes to minors, the regulation could not withstand a constitutional challenge.[28]

The Movie Rating System

The American movie classification system, unlike most classification systems throughout the world, is a voluntary, industry-run system.[29] Classification decisions are made by the Motion Picture Association of America's (MPAA) Code Administration and Rating Board. Although neither content nor treatment is banned or prohibited, there are several guidelines for filmmakers to heed if they covet a particular rating. The classifications include: G (General Audiences), PG (Parental Guidance Suggested, some material may not be suitable for children), PG-13 (Parents Strongly Cautioned, some material may be inappropriate for children under thirteen), R (Restricted, under seventeen requires accompanying parent or adult guardian), and NC-17, formerly the X rating (No Children under seventeen admitted). The MPAA did not register the X rating as a trademark. It can therefore be self-applied by pornographers without the approval of the board. The criteria used in ratings include drug use, nudity, language, sexual activity, and, to a lesser degree, violence. For example, drug use warrants at least a PG-13 rating. One sexually explicit word in the film automatically places it in the PG-13 category, and two guarantees an R rating. Brief nudity may earn a PG-13 rating; more extensive nudity during simulated sex will always earn a film at least an R rating if not an NC-17 rating.

Half of the 10,870 films reviewed by the MPAA since 1968 have received R or X/NC-17 ratings.[30] Exceptions to these guidelines require a unanimous vote of the board. A filmmaker who objects to the assigned rating has the option of editing and resubmitting the film to the board or appealing the rating to the Appeals Board. A two-thirds vote is necessary to override the initial decision, but as Richard Heffner, past chairman of the board, reported in 1987, reversals are successful as much as half the time.[31]

The ratings, however, go largely unenforced.[32] Youngsters twelve to seventeen comprise 17 percent of movie audiences, with 43 percent of them frequenting cinemas monthly.[33] Since there are few pressures to impose strict identification requirements at the box office, the financial incentives for theaters to ignore the MPAA ratings often prevail. Even if the theaters enforce the ratings, youngsters are allowed to view some of the most violent fare if they are accompanied by an adult. There simply is no legal mandate that theaters or video stores enforce the ratings.

Public Opinion

A 1987 nationwide survey found that three-quarters of the adults polled favored revision of the classification system to better reflect the amount of sex, violence, and profanity in American films, and 92 percent of those polled agreed that video stores should enforce the film ratings attached to videotapes and not rent or sell R, NC-17, or unrated films to minors.[34] While Americans go through periods of vocal opposition to sexually explicit and violent media, Hollywood's strength and the Supreme Court's interpretation of the First Amendment have stymied the efforts of groups that remain supportive of tougher restrictions on violent and sexually explicit materials.

Americans' approval of sexually explicit materials shows a complex trend.[35] Objections to various sexual presentations diminished in the early 1970s, but by the mid-1970s attitudes turned against pornography. Support for ending all laws regulating pornography declined, and belief in the negative effects of pornography grew. In the 1980s, there was little change. On some items, Americans became slightly more liberal. On others they became more conservative. Viewing of X-rated movies showed its own unique pattern. Viewing declined between 1973 and 1978. Then from 1978 to 1987, due to the increased use of VCRs, the viewing of X-rated movies climbed rapidly. In 1988 and 1989, viewing declined again. Meanwhile, Americans' attitudes toward other sexual issues have changed dramatically. There has been an increase in approval of premarital sex and cohabitation, sex education, and birth control.[36] On other issues, there has been less movement. Since the early 1970s there appears to have been no liberal shift, and even some conservative movement, in attitudes toward homosexuality, extramarital sex, and pornography.[37] In the early 1980s, a number of liberal trends slowed down and some reversed. The conservative shift, however, was modest. By the 1990s, views shifted once again toward liberalization, especially among students. For example, between 1969 and 1973, Americans have found nudity in Broadway plays, pictures of nude women, and topless waitresses less objectionable.[38] Between 1970 and 1989, however, the number of people who agreed with the statement that "Sexual materials provide information about sex" declined almost 5 percent to 56.9 percent, and concern about a breakdown in morals increased by close to 7 percent to 62.5 percent.[39] At least 10 percent more (59.9 percent) people in 1989 believed that sexual materials lead to sexual violence than did in 1970, but a staggering 25 percent more (60 percent) agreed that sexual materials provided an outlet for bottled-up impulses.[40]

A more recent study, however, found that only 47.2 percent perceived a link between sex crimes and pornography with 39.9 percent disagreeing and 11.6 percent undecided.[41] This recent study also reported that 51.5 percent of Americans approve of pornography's availability in bookstores, 55.2 percent approve of pornography's availability in video stores, and 83.1 percent believe that the government should not interfere in sexual relations between private consenting adults.[42]

Other sources report that Americans continue to support more restrictions on X-rated theaters, adult bookstores, and massage parlors, with as many as 40 percent believing pornography should be restricted regardless of age, effectively banning the material.[43] Almost two-thirds of the public was concerned with this situation and believed that such material affected community morality.[44] A small percentage of Americans believe pornography is such a serious crime that they call for the death penalty or castration for those who distribute and produce pornography.[45]

So while some sources report growing support for more regulations, others report increasing levels of tolerance. It is probably likely that the more recent trend is toward more tolerance, though the 2000 election results indicate continued opposition to homosexuality. This truth may be more complex with people generally becoming more tolerant of alternative lifestyles, particularly between heterosexuals, while holding significant distaste, at least publicly, for homosexuals and fetish-type behaviors. There can be no doubt that the public is divided on the issue but also supportive of strong constitutional protections for sexually explicit materials.

On the other hand, support may be growing for restricting sexual violence in films and magazines.[46] In 1986, as many as 73 percent wanted a ban on the sale or rental of videocassettes displaying sexual violence, up 10 points from the year before.[47] Seventy-four percent wanted to ban theaters that feature movies depicting sexual violence, and 73 percent wanted a ban on magazines that show sexual violence.[48]

The public, however, is more liberal when it comes to the presentation of nonviolent sex, but here, too, there has been an increase in favor of community restrictions. Fewer than half of Americans favored a ban on magazines or videos that show nudity or adults having sexual relations, but more people in 1986 favored some restrictions on these materials than did respondents in 1985.[49] In 2000, 45 percent say local standards should be tougher, compared to 5 percent who say they should be less strict. Forty-three percent feel they should be kept as they are now. Little change in views has occurred on this question from two earlier surveys.

The survey also revealed a close division of opinion on whether there should be a single nationwide standard in determining obscenity or whether each community should set its own standards. But only 7 percent feel there should be no standards whatsoever.[50] Sharp differences, however, were recorded on the basis of age, with the eighteen- to twenty-nine-year-olds holding far more liberal views than their elders, and Catholics consistently more liberal than Protestants, largely because of the conservative positions held by

Protestant evangelicals.[51] In general, those who are inclined toward suppression are likely to be older and less educated and to belong to a fundamentalist religious group.[52] Educational levels and participation in religious activities affect males' attitudes more than females' attitudes. A strong majority of Americans, 92 percent, support a ban on the sale or rental of material featuring sexual acts involving children.

Americans of both sexes believe that pornography has negative effects, including the beliefs that pornography dehumanizes women and that it causes men and women to lose respect for one another.[53] These respondents, however, believe that exposure to pornography affects other people's behavior more than it does their own. Despite this belief, nearly two-thirds believe that pornographic materials should be protected by the First Amendment.[54] Interestingly, those who perceived pornography to have the greatest effects, including deleterious effects on interpersonal relations between the sexes and violation of women's civil rights, were opposed to increased regulation.[55]

Although women dislike pornography, believe that there is a relationship between pornography and violence against women, and are concerned about the welfare of women, many also believe that legislation would lead to greater repression of women and that women have more to lose by censorship.[56] Other feminists see the issue from a complex political viewpoint: pornography is symbolic of women's inequality and partly responsible for their oppressed status. Still, a greater proportion of women simply see pornography as presenting women in uncharacteristic and inappropriate roles that appeal to men's sexual instincts.[57] Pornography features women misrepresenting how women really behave. Therefore, American women are more supportive of anti-pornography legislation and tend to agree more strongly that pornography is an important community issue.[58] Indeed, sex is the largest predictor of attitudes toward the regulation of pornography and the perceived effects of exposure to pornography with women being more supportive of regulation and more sensitive to pornography's real or imagined effect on its viewers.[59] Older women are the strongest advocates of traditional measures aimed at regulating pornography. These women do not see as much pornography and tend to react negatively to what they do see.[60]

CANADA

In spite of Canada's explicit protection of freedom of expression in the Canadian Charter of Rights, the Supreme Court of Canada held that the regulation of pornography is constitutionally permissible.[61] Adopting a civil rights approach to pornography, the Canadian Supreme Court moved away from the idea that obscenity laws exist to protect public morality and accepted the contention that obscenity is as much an equality issue as it is a freedom of expression issue.

Legal Approaches

Section 2 of the charter states: Everyone has the following fundamental freedoms: (a) freedom of conscience and religion; (b) freedom of thought, belief, opinion, and expression, including freedom of the press and other media of communication; (c) freedom of peaceful assembly; and (d) freedom of association.[62] The charter also contains an express provision allowing laws to violate protected rights and freedoms if the laws present "reasonable limits as can be demonstrably justified in a free and democratic society."[63] When a law is challenged under the charter, a court must first consider whether the law infringes a protected right or freedom and then, if so, whether the infringement can be justified under section 1. The section 1 analysis may take into account a wide range of legal, economic, and social considerations.

To establish that a limit is reasonably and demonstrably justified in a free and democratic society, two criteria must be satisfied. First, the limiting measures must be "of sufficient importance to warrant overriding a constitutionally protected right or freedom."[64] It is necessary, at a minimum, that an objective be "pressing and substantial" before it can be characterized as sufficiently important.[65] Second, once a sufficiently significant objective is recognized, the government must show that the means chosen are reasonably and demonstrably justified. This involves the application of the "proportionality test."[66]

The next stage of inquiry is a consideration of the means chosen by Parliament to achieve that objective. According to *R v. Oakes*, the proportionality requirement under section 1 consists of three components: the existence of a rational connection between the impugned measures and the objective, minimal impairment of the right of freedom; and a proper balance between the effects of the limiting measures and the legislative objective. Justice Sopinka stated in *Butler* that pornography does not stand on an equal footing with other kinds of expression that are at the "core" of freedom of expression values, such as the search for truth and individual self-fulfillment.[67] He therefore held in *Butler* that, while a direct link between obscenity and harm may be difficult (if not impossible) to establish, Parliament was entitled to conclude that exposure to images bears a causal relationship to changes in attitudes and beliefs.

Butler involved the application of section 163 of the Canadian Criminal Code to hard-core pornography. Section 163 controls the dissemination of obscene material. It states:

(1) Every one commits an offence who, (a) makes, prints, publishes, distributes, circulates, or has in his possession for the purpose of publication, distribution or circulation any obscene written matter, picture, model, phonograph record or other thing whatever. . . . (2) Every one commits an offence who knowingly, without lawful justification or excuse, (a) sells, exposes to public view or has in his possession for such a purpose any obscene written matter, picture, model, phonograph record or other thing whatever, (b) publicly exhibits a disgusting object or an indecent show . . . (8) for the purposes of this Act, any publication a dominant characteristic of which is the undue exploitation of sex, or of sex and any one or more of the following subjects, namely, crime, horror, cruelty, and violence, shall be deemed to be obscene.[68]

The court noted that the statute encompassed three categories of material: "(1) explicit sex with violence, (2) explicit sex without violence but which subjects people to treatment that is degrading or dehumanizing, and (3) explicit sex without violence that is neither degrading nor dehumanizing."[69] The court repeated that the harm that could result from the material served as a benchmark for determining the community's tolerance of the material. The court wrote that harm in this context encompassed material "that . . . predisposes persons to act in an antisocial manner."[70] The stronger the inference of a risk of harm, the lesser the likelihood of tolerance.[71] Referring back to the three categories, the Court held that sex with violence will "almost always constitute the undue exploitation of sex," and explicit, degrading sex may constitute undue exploitation if "the risk of harm is substantial."[72] However, explicit sex that is not dehumanizing is tolerable "unless it employs children in its production."[73]

Like American courts, the Canadian Supreme Court has developed a community standards test.[74] But the Canadian test is based on what the Canadian community would tolerate other Canadians being exposed to.[75] At least one recent case has found that material that is "degrading or dehumanizing" is a violation of this standard.[76] Accordingly, the Canadian Supreme Court has allowed regulation and censorship of "publications which degrade people by linking violence, cruelty, or other forms of dehumanizing treatment with sex."[77] This regulation is allowed on the grounds that the material "degrades the human dimensions of life to a subhuman or merely physical dimension and thereby contributes to a process of moral desensitization and must be harmful in some way. It must therefore be controlled when it gets out of hand, [or] when it becomes 'undue.'"[78]

To protect artistic, political, literary, and scientific speech, the Canadian Supreme Court has also adopted an "internal necessities" test aimed at protecting works that contain "exploitative sex" when it is "required in the serious treatment of the theme of [an artistic work] with honesty and uprightness." This rule is aimed at narrowing the focus of the "undue exploitation" test to those representations which are merely "dirt for dirt's sake."[79] If a work contains sexually explicit material that, by itself, would constitute the undue exploitation of sex, then the portrayal of sex must be viewed as a whole to determine the dominant theme of the work. If, however, sex is the main object of the work, and the work lacks a wider artistic, literary, or other value, then the work is an undue exploitation of sex under the regulation. In *Time Square Cinema Ltd.*, Jessup J. A. held that a correct charge to the jury on the issue of obscenity would instruct the jury to have regard for the following three factors: (1) the purpose of the producer, (2) the artistic merit of the work, and (3) the community standards of tolerance.[80]

In determining that certain forms of pornography can be restricted, and even banned, the Canadian Supreme Court deferred to

Parliament.[81] The court held that Parliament could conclude that 163(8) was necessary to prevent identifiable harms to society analogous to that of hate propaganda.[82] Under section 1 of the charter, restrictions on free expression are permissible when the harm caused by the proliferation of materials seriously offends the values fundamental to Canadian society.[83] The court recognized several harms associated with the dissemination of pornography, stating that pornography reinforces male-female stereotypes to the detriment of both sexes. It attempts to make degradation, humiliation, victimization, and violence in human relationships appear normal and acceptable. The *Butler* court also stated that there is public concern that the exploitation of women and children depicted in publications and films can sometimes lead to "abject and servile victimization."[84] Justice Anderson, concurring in *Regina v. Red Hot Video*, argued that if we are to achieve equality between men and women, it is wrong to "ignore the threat to equality resulting from exposure to an audience of certain types of violent and degrading material. Materials portraying women as a class as objects for sexual exploitation and abuse has a negative impact on woman's sense of self-worth"[85] and poses a "threat to equality."[86]

The court pointed out that similar legislation was found in most free and democratic societies.[87] The court also held that the legislation was consistent with Canada's international law obligations under the Agreement for the Suppression of the Circulation of Obscene Publications and the Convention for the Suppression of the Circulation of Traffic in Obscene Publications.[88] Finally, the court wrote that "the burgeoning pornography industry renders [Parliament's] concern even more pressing and substantial than when [the legislation was] first enacted."[89] "A society which holds that egalitarianism, nonviolence, consensualism, and mutuality are basic to any human interaction, whether sexual or other, is clearly justified in controlling and prohibiting any medium of depiction, description or advocacy which violates these principles."[90]

Therefore, unlike American courts, the Canadian Supreme Court held: "[W]hile a direct link between obscenity and harm may be difficult, if not impossible to establish, it is reasonable to presume that exposure to images bears a causal relationship to changes in attitudes and beliefs."[91] Therefore, the court found that "a sufficiently rational link [exists] between the criminal sanction . . . [the] community's disapproval of the dissemination of materials which potentially victimize women and the negative influence that such materials have on changes in attitudes and behavior."[92]

The court held that the infringement on the freedom of expression did not outweigh the legislative objective in regulating pornography.[93] On the other hand, section 163 did not "proscribe sexually explicit erotica without violence that is not degrading or dehumanizing."[94] Its goal is simply "to catch material that creates a risk of harm to society."[95] By adopting a harm-based equality interpretation, the court made certain the law could be more predictably applied than if it had concluded that "undue exploitation of sex" included mere explicitness. The law would then probably have been too vague to apply consistently.[96]

Materials that have scientific, artistic, or literary merit are not captured by the provision. Further, only the public distribution and exhibition of obscene materials is at issue.[97] In reaching this balance, the court found that there is no less intrusive alternative to the criminalization of pornography.[98] The court also stated that it would "not, in the name of minimal impairment, take a restrictive approach to social science evidence and require legislatures to choose the least ambitious means to protect vulnerable groups."[99]

In sum, the court held that section 163 imposed a burden on expression, but the burden was justified because of its effects on promoting equality and preventing serious harm to society. Therefore, the provision was saved by section 1 of the Canadian Charter, which requires that the rights and freedoms of the people of Canada be subject "only to such reasonable limits prescribed by law as can be demonstrably justified in a free and democratic society."[100]

Public Opinion

Canada has made a strong commitment to the ideal of equality. This commitment is embodied in section 15 of the charter, which stipulates: "[E]very individual is equal before and under the law and has the right to the equal protection and equal benefit of the law without discrimination and, in particular, without discrimination based on race, national or ethnic origin, color, religion, sex, age, or mental or physical disability."[101] Section 15 of the Canadian Charter is much broader in scope than the Fourteenth Amendment to the American Constitution since it has wider substantive protections and more prohibited grounds of discrimination. Although equality is a protected right, the U.S. legal system does not make a similar commitment to the concept of egalitarianism as the Canadian legal and human rights culture does. American equality law focuses much more on the notion of equality of opportunity as opposed to the idea of equality of condition embraced by the Canadian Charter. For example, the court found that hate speech laws were constitutionally valid because, by creating such laws, Parliament had sought to "bolster the notion of mutual respect necessary in a nation which venerates the equality of all persons."[102] Likewise, Canadians are perceived to support a stronger stand in favor of law and order.[103]

Unlike pornography, simple possession of child pornography is an offense punishable by imprisonment for up to five years.[104] The Canadian Supreme Court made it clear that explicit child pornography is a special category of obscene material under section 163. A producer of a video depicting explicit sexual intercourse involving a fourteen-year-old could be convicted under the Child Pornography Law or under section 163. The difference is in the sentence: up to ten years' imprisonment under the Child Pornography Law, but only up to two years under section 163.

In the early 1980s the federal government commissioned a number of studies on child pornography. While the reports of both committees recommended legislative action to deal with child pornography, both also conceded that there was no empirical support for the claim that large amounts of child pornography were being consumed in Canada. Indeed, both committees found that there was little child pornography in Canada. Whatever did exist was imported.[105]

A recent comprehensive study on child sexual abuse stated that a conservative estimate of the annual incidence of such abuse involving physical contact is 7.3 per thousand, or about 16,500 children in Ontario alone.[106] It is relevant that the age of consent to sexual relations under the code is generally fourteen.[107] Where the other person is in a position of trust or authority or is a person with whom the young person is in a relationship of dependency, the age of consent

to sexual relations is eighteen.[108] The age of consent to anal intercourse is eighteen for unmarried persons.[109] Although Canada's age
of consent laws allow people to have sex at age fourteen, child
pornography laws prevent any photographs being taken of nude
teens until they turn eighteen, even if they consent to them.[110] The
court easily found the objective to protect children from sexual
abuse sufficiently important to warrant overriding to some degree
the constitutionally protected right or freedom.

CONCLUSION (UNITED STATES AND CANADA)

Canada and the United States, despite their proximity, have taken
different approaches to pornography. Canada's civil rights approach
indicates a commitment to equality of condition, where the United
States's libertarian approach prioritizes freedom. Additionally,
pornography is a major industry in the United States. This is largely
an outgrowth of the entertainment industry, but it also says something about American culture. The United States is not nearly as puritan as some pornography proponents argue. Instead, the United
States is one of the more liberal nations in the world.

The proliferation of pornography throughout the United States, and
the proliferation of violent movies, may have taken its toll. The
United States has one of the highest rates of violent crime among
western democracies. Recognizing pornography as low-value speech,
Canada prioritizes women's rights over the rights of pornographers
and pornography users. Canada's restrictiveness, however, could negatively affect Canada's sexual minorities by criminalizing or discour-
aging discussion about alternative lifestyles, but Canada's commitment to equality should counteract any tendency toward intolerance
among Canadians, usually a tolerant and compassionate people.

AUSTRALIA

Australia, like other Western nations, went through a sexual revolution in the 1960s, which led to a lessening of restrictions on sexually
explicit materials. At the same time, the regulation of pornography

has not generated as much controversy as it has in other Western nations. For example, Britain (Williams Commission), the United States (Johnson and Meese Commissions), and Canada (Fraser Commission) have at one time or another established national commissions to study the issue of pornography. The current trend, however, is toward more restriction, particularly in regard to protecting children and eliminating violence. As in many Western countries, except the United States, violent materials are considered more dangerous than nonviolent sexually explicit materials. Indeed, even among pornography users there exists agreement that violent media should be restricted to adults-only sections of video stores. R-rated videos are currently restricted to adults eighteen and over. This shows that the toleration for pornography is not based primarily on the libertarian view that adults should be able to view whatever they want or on freedom of speech grounds as much as it is on the view that, unlike violent materials, nonviolent sexually explicit materials simply aren't terribly harmful when viewed by consenting adults.

When it comes to protecting children, Australia is currently developing a rating system for video games and a policy for the regulation of the Internet. The main goals of Internet regulation are to protect children from sexually explicit websites, to restrict violent materials, and to ban child pornography. In this regard, Australia is about as restrictive as most European nations. In the end, violence, rather than sexual content, is the target of many of its restrictions.

The availability of pornography in Australia is quite open.[111] The sex-video industry in Australia is estimated to be worth $35 million a year.[112] Pornography and other adult products are available in sex shops, newsstands, supermarkets, and gas stations throughout the country.[113] Current catalogues of X-rated video distributors located in Canberra, the porn capital of Australia, sell a wide range of pornography, including ritual bondage and anal sex.[114] Before 1983 there were no laws governing the sale or distribution of sexually explicit videos in Australia.[115] There have, however, been pornography and obscenity laws on the books from much earlier time periods.[116]

Between 1876 and 1902, each state or colony in Australia passed obscenity legislation modeled on the British Act of 1857 and incorporated *Hicklin*, the first legal definition of obscenity.[117] Under *Hicklin*, "the test for obscenity is . . . whether the tendency of the matter . . . is to deprave and corrupt those whose minds are open to such immoral influences and into whose hands a publication of this sort may fall."[118] Most Australian colonies during this period suppressed the dissemination of "indecent" literature, as opposed to obscene or pornographic material as we know it today.

After the territories formed a federation in 1901, state laws against obscene and indecent material were supplemented by a range of new federal laws and regulations which aimed to prevent the importation of "questionable" material and to establish censorship regimes.[119] In general, film has attracted more stringent censorship provisions than printed publications while, within this latter category, "high art" literary publications have been dealt with much more leniently.[120]

During the prosperous era of the mid-1940s to the early 1950s, a new sexual culture began to emerge, one that emphasized different patterns of sexual interaction.[121] The pursuit of sexual pleasure, both inside and outside marriage, became more popular.[122] The increased availability of abortion and contraception and the increasing deployment of sexual themes in popular literature facilitated the change. Reinforcing this pattern, the stationing of foreign troops on Australian soil during World War II had the effect of sexualizing the local female population.[123]

Legal Approaches

As in the United States, the 1960s became a period of sexual liberation in Australia. Even though pornography was prohibited, support grew among many parliamentarians for the argument that adult literature should be relatively free of oppressive censorship controls.[124] In 1967, Parliament amended the Obscene and Indecent Publications Act. The amendment restricted publications that, in the opinion of the minister and on the advice of the State Advisory Committee, gave undue emphasis to sex, drug addiction, crimes of violence, gross cruelty or horror, or otherwise had a tendency to deprave, corrupt, or injure the morals of any person, class of persons, or age groups, or were undesirable reading for children under the age of sixteen.[125] These restricted publications were to be sold within adult-only shops and could not be exhibited to public view.[126]

While a largely uniform approach to the regulation of sexually explicit material now exists across Australia, X-rated videos can be sold only in the Australian Capital Territory and the Northern Territory.[127] Child pornography and materials depicting nonconsensual sexual violence are prohibited.[128] Television channels in Australia are obligated to specify their program content. A typical TV guide in Australia would include classifications such as PG (Parental Guidance), which means nudity free, and M (Mature)—formerly AO (Adults Only)—which may have seminudity, full frontal nudity, and sex scenes.[129] In 1983, the federal government introduced a uniform videotape classification scheme that some believe may be the "world's best practice model for video classification systems."[130]

Legislation introduced in February 1984 included the X classification. The task of determining X-rated films and print materials fell to the Film Censorship Board. This body reviews and rates all legal films shown or distributed in Australia, as well as classifying certain print materials. The board's recommendations are based on three principles: (1) adults should be able to read, see, and hear what they wish in private and in public; (2) children must be adequately protected from material likely to harm or disturb them; and (3) people should be protected from exposure to unsolicited material they find offensive.[131] Australia bans violence, coercion, "offensive fetishes," and depictions that "debase or abuse."[132] The sexual behaviors allowed in the X category in the original formulation included "All depictions of sexual acts involving adults (except those of an extreme sexually violent or cruel nature) including explicit penetration, masturbation, ejaculations, fellation, cunnilingus, insertion of objects in orifices, urolagnia, necrophilia, coprophilia, sadomasochism, and fetishism."[133] In December of 1984, the formulation was revised to include "Material which includes explicit depictions of sexual acts involving adults, but does not include any depiction suggesting coercion or non-consent of any kind."[134]

The classification scheme became compulsory throughout Australia by June 1984. All videos available for sale in Australia had to be classified by the Film Censorship Board. While the classification process was the province of the federal government, states could refuse to allow the sale of categories of videos within their own borders. As a result, the sale of X-rated videos became illegal outside the Australian Capital Territory and the Northern Territory in 1985.[135]

Each territory has attempted to drive the X-rated video industry from its jurisdiction. For example, the Australian Capital Territory attempted to do so through taxation, and the Northern Territory by restricting aspects of the video distribution process. While the sale of such materials throughout much of Australia is severely restricted, the mail-order delivery of X-rated videos remains unrestricted. In other words, the interstate sale of videos by mail is legal.[136]

In January 1996, the Film Censorship Board changed its name to the Official Film Classification Board, dropping the term "censorship," and modified the X rating. The X rating was changed to allow videos which (a) explicitly depict sexual activity between adults, where there is no sexual violence, coercion, or nonconsent of any kind, in a way that is likely to cause offense to a reasonable adult; and (b) are unsuitable for a minor to see.[137] A film can be refused classification if it contains:

> depictions of child sexual abuse, bestiality, sexual acts accompanied by offensive fetishes, or exploitative incest fantasies, unduly detailed and/or relished acts of extreme violence or cruelty; explicit or unjustifiable depictions of sexual violence against non-consenting persons, or detailed instruction or encouragement in: (i) matters of crime or violence, or (ii) the abuse of [illegal] drugs.[138]

> Videos may also be banned if they:

> a. depict, express or otherwise deal with matters of sex, drug misuse or addiction, crime, cruelty, violence or revolting or abhorrent phenomena in such a way that they offend against the standards of morality, decency and propriety generally accepted by reasonable adults to the extent that they should not be classified; or
> b. depict, in a way that is likely to cause offence to a reasonable adult, a minor who is, or who appears to be, under 16 (whether or not engaged in sexual activity); or
> c. promote, incite or instruct in matters of crime or violence.[139]

The censors may refuse to classify print material if it contains pictorial representations of "bestiality," "child pornography including exploitative nudity," or "extreme cruelty and dangerous practices."[140]

Written descriptions may also be denied classification if they are deemed to promote, incite, or encourage crimes, violence, or drug abuse, including "do it yourself" and "growers manuals." The classifiers may also reject written materials that present the "relishment or detailed descriptions of gratuitous acts of cruelty," the "detailed or unjustifiable descriptions of sexual violence against non-consenting persons," or "gratuitous descriptions of sexual activity involving persons under 16 years of age."[141] Any hint of violence, even "playful slapping on the bum," can render the video unclassifiable, effectively banned, unless the video specifically states it features "mild" bondage or sadomasochism. If a film or print work is denied classification, it is not legally available for sale in Australia. Classification decisions may be appealed to the Film and Literature Board of Review.[142]

The guidelines classify the materials into two categories. Category 1 materials are available to persons eighteen years old and over and must be displayed in sealed wrappers.[143] This category allows pictorial representations of "explicit nudity," "implied depictions of sexual acts," "obscured depictions of sexual acts," "mild fetishes," "artwork, cartoons, etc. . . . depicting realistic explicit nudity or sexual activity," and "realistic and explicit depictions of violence or its aftermath, except if extremely cruel or violent."[144] Acceptable written materials may include "realistic and gratuitous descriptions of violence" and "relished descriptions of sexual activity involving adults." Magazines such as *Penthouse*, *Playboy*, *Mayfair*, and other "adult" magazines fit this classification, as do many mainstream novels.

Category 2 materials are also available to persons eighteen years and greater but may only be sold on "restricted premises," such as adult shops.[145] The allowable contents in these materials include pictorial depictions of "explicit sexual acts" and "fetishes including sadomasochism and bondage if not extreme."[146] Written descriptions may include "descriptions of sexual activity including activity between humans and animals."[147]

The Restricted rating allows depictions where "sexual intercourse or other sexual activity may be realistically implied or simulated."[148] The R-rated material is restricted to adults eighteen years and over. It is defined as "Material considered likely to be harmful to those under eighteen years and/or possibly offensive to some sections of the adult community."[149] The key difference between the R rating and the X rating is the "explicit" depiction of sexual activity. This difference involves whether the "pistons and cylinders" are shown in action. Generally, the penis cannot be shown erect in an R-rated video. The Australian law on male nudity even specifies that in non-X-rated adult magazines, such as the *Australian Women's Forum*, which features male nude centerfolds, the male penis depicted must not "surpass a 45 degree angle of inclination."[150] Additionally, any digital or other manipulation of the clitoris or other parts of the vagina will push the video into X territory. Finally, excessive violence and foul language, especially the F-word, will earn a film the R rating.[151] The R rating is the highest rating allowed to be shown publicly in the states outside the territories.[152]

During the 1990s, pornography continued to attract significant public and political attention in Australia. Debates continued about the regulation of X-rated videos and the depiction of violence in film and television.[153] The period between 1991 and 1993 saw a flurry of activity with regard to attempts to either ban or limit the production and distribution of pornographic materials.[154] For example, the Queensland Labor government voted to accept the classification scheme developed by the federal government but banned the sale of X-rated videos and category 1 and 2 publications within its borders. In 1992 the Northern Territory government moved to restrict the production and duplication of X-rated videos within its borders. Registered companies could reproduce no more than one-hundred copies of any X-rated title in a given year.[155] This effectively eliminated pornography production in the Northern Territory.

These changes have been surprisingly uncontroversial, indicating a political consensus regarding the regulation of pornography. Whether this consensus is temporary or contingent remains to be seen. In the wake of feminist and conservative critiques of pornography in the 1980s, there appears to be widespread acceptance of the need to prohibit certain sorts of pornography. In the 1990s, new areas of unanimity appear to have emerged. Parliamentarians generally avoided sexual libertarianism and concurred on the need to prohibit the distribution of material which depicted nonconsensual sexual violence.[156] We do not see parliamentarians defending the rights of pornography consumers or suggesting that the use of pornography is a harmless and/or legitimate expression of a citizen's privacy. No parliamentarian has suggested that pornography is a useful outlet for those who are handicapped or too ugly to aspire to normal sexual relations. Also missing is the argument, central to libertarian discourse, that because representations are ideas rather than actions, reflecting rather than constructing the world, they should not be subject to government controls. Most parliamentarians accept that representations of violence, particularly sexual violence, need to be subject to stringent censorship guidelines. This new consensus around sexual violence clearly reflects the ongoing impact of anti-pornography feminism on Australian political discourse.[157] Indeed, it appears that there is now less public and political support for moves to extend the availability of pornography.[158]

The 1995 Classification Act included measures designed to generally extend censorship powers over publications, films, and videos. It is notable that these measures were relatively uncontroversial in Parliament, particularly in comparison to the situation in 1971, when the R classification for films was introduced, and in 1983 through 1984, when video regulation was debated.[159] More recently, the commonwealth, states, and territories agreed to change the X rating. The new nonviolent erotica category would ban violence, coercion, "sexually assaultive language," "demeaning" depictions, and a range of fetishes.[160] The government of Prime Minister John Howard, which introduced the legislation in 1999, said that the category change would fulfill its 1996 election promise to ban X-rated videos.[161] Finally, new measures to classify and restrict the distribution of computer games and the availability of pornography over the Internet were also widely supported by parliamentarians from all political parties. The concern here was that children were being exposed to inappropriate violence and sexual violence. Consequently, few voices were raised in opposition to the imposition of tougher control on computer games than on publications, films, and videos.

Self-regulation, supplemented by codes of conduct and some new criminal law, has been proposed to deal with the transmission of pornography on the Internet and via computer bulletin boards.[162] The proposed strategy for regulation of the Internet uses a self-regulatory framework incorporating a code of practice and a complaints-handling procedure. Self-regulation means that there will be no attempt to classify material accessed through on-line information services. A comprehensive education program will assist parents and teachers to protect children from unsuitable material. New offense provisions will be introduced to provide sanctions against persons who "deliberately breach community standards" in relation to on-line services.[163]

More recently, the government has threatened to close down some Australia-based websites. Under Australia's Broadcasting Services Act, locally hosted websites that are, or even would be, rated X can be issued a takedown notice by the Australian Broadcasting Authority.[164] The Australian Broadcasting Authority will be given the power to follow up on complaints and order Internet providers in Australia with illegal or X-rated material on their servers to remove it. Australian sites will not be allowed to include material which would earn an R rating unless mechanisms are in place to keep children away from the sites. Overseas sites, which make up the bulk of pornography on the Internet, will be self-regulated. Internet providers are expected to take reasonable steps to block access to the sites.[165]

Public Opinion

One recent study demonstrated the extent of the consensus among Australians about the need to regulate pornography. Hugh Potter conducted a survey of pornography users in 1992.[166] While this self-selected sample is by no means representative of the views of the general public of Australia, some of the results indicated that even Australian pornography users support the current regulatory scheme. The study used what Potter called a "theoretical sampling."[167] A total of 1,887 survey forms were used. Twenty percent, or 380, of the survey forms were returned in usable condition.[168] Potter put a number of statements into the survey. He asked the respondents to classify their answers on a five-point scale, from "strongly disagree" to "strongly agree." Among other things, the survey found that porn users generally had higher educational levels and incomes. Potter also concluded that the survey revealed that the respondents were more liberal or tolerant in their social attitudes than the average Australian.[169] The responses relevant to this survey are described below.

In 1991 and 1992 there were moves by some groups in Australia to have R-rated videos held in separate, adults-only sections of video stores. Potter put this opinion statement into his survey: "R-rated films should be kept in an adults-only section of video shops." Seventy-nine percent agreed or strongly agreed with the statement.[170] This response indicates that restricting R-rated videos, which tend to contain more violence than sex, is acceptable even among porn users.

The controversy over the display of "adult" (category 1) magazines led Potter to pose this statement to the respondents: "Adult magazines (e.g., *Playboy*) should be kept in sealed packages with only the title displayed." Fifty-seven percent of the respondents either agreed or strongly agreed. Relatively few strongly disagreed. The respondent's sex was significantly associated with the type of response given. Women proportionately placed themselves at the "strongly agree" end while men tended to congregate in the middle.[171] The difference in the responses between female pornography users and male pornography users indicates a gender difference that may be cross-cultural. Women may be less comfortable with the ubiquitous public display of naked female bodies. The result also shows that Australian pornography users are comfortable with their nation's regulatory scheme.

In response to the statement "X-rated videos should be available in regular video rental shops" 65 percent agreed. While half of all the respondents chose to simply "agree," rather than "strongly agree," the disagreeing group was larger than expected.[172] This may indicate that pornography users are not particularly concerned with gaining access to pornography, as they may have sufficient access already.

When Potter put the statement "X-rated videos degrade all women" to the respondents, he again found a difference between the female respondents and the male respondents. While only 8 percent of the respondents supported the statement, Potter noted the strength of disagreement was again related to the respondent's sex. While 90 percent of the respondents checked either "disagree" or "strongly disagree" with the statement, more men (57 percent) than women

(35 percent) responded in the "strongly disagree" category. Potter found proportionately more women (59 percent) than men (35 percent) in the "disagree" category.[173] The female respondents, while not agreeing in general that pornography degrades women, tended not to disregard the statement as thoroughly as did the men.

Potter concluded that, even though his study represented mostly middle-class and upper-middle-class pornography users, findings strongly contradicted those studies using university students in their early adult years. He did not find that pornography had any significant detrimental influence on its users.[174] Potter also concluded that there was a large area of agreement in regard to restricting pornography and that the Australian people did not seem to be terribly concerned about nonviolent sexually explicit videos.[175]

Approaches to Prostitution

The widespread adoption of tougher criminal penalties for street prostitution, even in those jurisdictions where decriminalization is being introduced, has been seen by some as further evidence of the emergence of a new conservative consensus.[176] Australia now has a more diverse set of prostitution laws than any other country in the world;[177] there are marked differences in the laws pertaining to prostitution across Australia. While different types of decriminalization have taken place in some jurisdictions, the laws pertaining to prostitution in South Australia, Tasmania, and Western Australia have remained virtually unchanged since the beginning of the twentieth century. In Queensland there is now a more extensive regime of criminal penalties attached to prostitution than in any other state at any other time. South Australia, in 1995, and Queensland, in 1992, have both introduced new anti-prostitution laws. In four other jurisdictions—the Australian Capital Territory, the Northern Territory, Victoria, and New South Wales—some form of decriminalization has been introduced. In the Australian Capital Territory brothels are now legal if they are registered and located outside residential areas. In the Northern Territory, escort agencies are subject to licensing but are otherwise legal. Brothels remain illegal. Victoria in 1995 extended its system of regulated brothels to include escort agencies, and New South Wales established clearer grounds for the legal operation of brothels.

There even appears to be a general shift to broader definitions of prostitution regardless of whether decriminalization has also occurred. In both the Australian Capital Territory and Queensland, for example, the law now specifies that prostitution can include acts of masturbation and sexual voyeurism where no physical contact occurs. Further attempts at decriminalization have failed.[178] Even parliamentarians who are supportive of decriminalization are now unambivalent about also supporting tough criminal laws against street prostitution.[179]

CONCLUSION (AUSTRALIA)

Some have argued that the settlement of Australia subjected women to an "enforced whoredom."[180] Initially, England used Australia as a penal settlement. In order to survive, women were forced to trade sexual services for food, shelter, and protection. From its inception, Australian society has assumed and enforced the prostitution of women. In regard to pornography, however, Australia remained true to its English roots. Pornography, though available, remained fairly restricted. Now, after a wave of sexual regulation, pornography remains widely available, but the trend has been toward restricting pornography to adults-only establishments, thereby balancing the public demand for sexually explicit materials with the public's concerns to protect children and prevent violence and drug use.

NOTES

1. Alix Sharkey, "The Guardian Weekend Page," *Guardian*, (Nov. 22, 1997).

2. Ernest Giglio, *Rights, Liberties, and Public Policy* (Brookfield, Vt.: Avebury, 1995).

3. Margeret E. Thompson, et al., "Regulating Pornography: A Public Dilemma" in *Journal of Communication* 73 (summer 1990).

4. Giglio, *Rights*, 168.

5. Jerome O'Callaghan, "Censorship of Indecency in Ireland: A View from Abroad," 16 *Cardozo Arts & Entertainment Law* 53, 75 n. 109 (1999).

6. U.S. Const. Amend. I.

7. U.S. Const. Amend. XIV.

8. Susan M. Easton, *The Problem of Pornography: Regulation and the Right to Free Speech* (New York: Routledge, 1994).

9. *Roth v. United States,* 354 U.S. 476, 485 (1957).

10. *R. v. Hicklin, LR 3QB 360 (1868).*

11. Kevin W. Saunders, "The United States and Canadian Responses to the Feminist Attack on Pornography: A Perspective from the History of Obscenity," 9 *Ind. Int'l & Comp. L. Rev.* 1 (1998).

12. *Roth,* 354 U.S., 487 n. 20.

13. Ibid.

14. Ibid.

15. Saunders, *United States and Canadian,* 14–15.

16. See *R.A.V. v. City of St. Paul,* 505 U.S. 377, 398–401 (White, J., concurring) (1992).

17. *Miller v. California,* 413 U.S. 15 (1973).

18. Ibid., 24.

19. Giglio, *Rights,* 165.

20. Janet Steele, "Banning Porn Curtails Freedom of Expression." *Jakarta Post,* (Sept. 16, 1999).

21. Catherine MacKinnon, "Pornography, Civil Rights, and Speech," 20 *Harv. Civ. Rts. & Civ. Lib. L. Rev.* 1 (1985); Michelle Chernikoff Anderson, "Speaking Freely about Reducing Violence against Women: A Harm Reduction Strategy from the Law and Social Science of Pornography," 10 *U. Fla. J.L. & Pub. Pol'y* 173 (1998).

22. *American Booksellers Ass'n v. Hudnut,* 771 F.2d 323, 327-32 (7th Cir. 1985) *(aff'd* 475 U.S. 1001) (1986).

23. See Marie-France Major, "Obscene Comparisons: Canadian and American Attitudes toward Pornography Regulation," 19 *J. Contemp. L.* 51, 74–75 (1993).

24. *New York v. Ferber,* 458 U.S. 747 (1982).

25. Ibid., 759.

26. *F.C.C. v. Pacifica,* 438 U.S. 726 (1978).

27. *Young v. American Mini Theaters* (1976); *Renton v. Playtime Theatres* (1986).

28. *Video Software Dealers Association v. Webster* (1991).

29. Giglio, *Rights,* 117.

30. Ibid., 177 (1995).

31. Ibid., 120.

32. Ibid., 133.

33. Ibid., 136.

34. Ibid., 135–36.

35. Tom W. Smith, "The Sexual Revolution," 54 *Public Opinion Quarterly* 415, 417 (Fall 1990).

36. Ibid., 419.

37. Ibid., 419.

38. Ibid.

39. Ibid.

40. Ibid.

41. Bohsiu Wu and Charles H. McCaghy, "Attitudinal Determinants of Public Opinions toward Legalized Pornography," 21 *Journal of Criminal Justice* 17 (1993).

42. Ibid., 17.

43. Smith, Sexual Revolution, 424.

44. Giglio, *Rights*, 111.

45. Wu and McCaghy, "Determinants," 13.

46. "Pornography: Growing Support Found for Ban on Sex Violence in Movies, Magazines," 251 *Gallup Report* 2 (Aug. 1986).

47. Ibid.

48. Ibid.

49. Ibid.

50. Ibid.

51. Ibid.

52. Wu and McCaghy, "Determinants," 14–15.

53. Thompson, "Regulating Pornography," 75–76.

54. Ibid., 80.

55. Ibid.

56. G. Cowan et al., "Feminist and Fundamentalist Attitudes toward Pornography Control," 13 *Psychol Women Quarterly* 97 (1989).

57. Wu and McCaghy, "Determinants," 26.

58. Thompson, "Regulating Pornography," 75–76.

59. Ibid.; Wu and McCaghy, "Determinants," 13.

60. Thompson, "Regulating Pornography," 81.

61. *Regina v. Butler,* 70 C.C.C. (3d) 129 (Can. 1992).

62. Can. Const. (Constitution Act, 1982) pt. I (Canadian Charter of Rights and Freedoms), 2.

63. Brian M. Blugerman, "Beyond Obscenity: Canada's New Child Pornography Law," 11 *WTR Ent. & Sports Law* 3, 8 (Winter, 1994).

64. *R. v. Big M Drug Mart Ltd.,* [1985] 1 S.C.R. 295.

65. *R. v. Oakes,* 138.

66. *Butler*, 139.

67. *Butler*, 499.

68. Marie-France Major, "Obscene Comparisons: Canadian and American Attitudes toward Pornography Regulation," 19 *J. Contemp. L.* 51, 80 (1993).

69. *Butler*, 70 C.C.C. (3d) at 150.

70. Ibid.

71. Ibid., 150–51.

72. Ibid., 151.

73. Ibid.

74. *Regina v. Brodie,* [1962] 1 S.C.R. 681 (Can.), 132 C.C.C. 161, 182 (Can. 1962).

75. *Regina v. Towne Cinema Theatres,* [1985] 1 S.C.R. 494 (Can.), 18 C.C.C. (3d) at 205.

76. *Regina v. Doug Rankine Co. Ltd.,* 9 C.C.C. (3d) 53, 90 (D. Ont. 1983).

77. *Towne Cinema Theatres,* [1985] 1 S.C.R. 494 (Can.), 18 C.C.C. (3d) at 203.

78. Ibid., 217–218 (Wilson, J., concurring).

79. *Butler,* 70 C.C.C. (3d) at 148–149 (citing *Brodie,* [1962] S.C.R. 681, 132 C.C.C. (3d) at 181; *Regina v. Odeon Morton Theatres Ltd.,* 45 D.L.R. (3d) 224 (Man. Ct. App. 1974), 16, C.C.C. (2d) 185 (1974)).

80. Bernadette Schell et al., "Development of a Pornography Community Standard: Questionnaire Results for Two Canadian Cities," 29 *Canadian J. Criminology* 133 (Apr. 1987).

81. Ibid., 155–60.

82. In *Regina v. Keegstra,* [1990] 3 S.C.R. 776, a case dealing with the constitutionality of the hate propaganda provisions of the Criminal Code, the Court concluded that the absence of proof of a causative link between hate propaganda and hatred of an identifiable group was not a determinative factor. The Court argued: First, to predicate the limitation of free expression upon proof of actual hatred gives insufficient attention to the severe psychological trauma suffered by members of those identifiable groups targeted by hate propaganda. Second, it is clearly difficult to prove a causative link between a specific statement and hatred of an identifiable group.

83. *Regina v. Keegstra* at 159.

84. Ibid. (quoting *Regina v. Red Hot Video Ltd.,* 18 C.C.C. (3d) 36, 43–44 (1985) (Nemetz, C.J.B.C., concurring)).

85. *Butler,* 70 C.C.C. (3d) at 159 (citing *Red Hot Video,* 18 C.C.C. (3d) at 8 [Anderson, J., concurring]).

86. *Butler,* 70 C.C.C. (3d) at 159 (citing *Red Hot Video,* 18 C.C.C. (3d) at 8).

87. Ibid., 159.

88. Ibid., 160.

89. Ibid.

90. Ibid., 157 (quoting *Report on Pornography by the Standing Committee on Justice and Legal Affairs* 18:4 [1978]).

91. Ibid., 163.

92. Ibid., 164.

93. Ibid., 168.

94. Ibid., 165.

95. Ibid.

96. Ibid., n183.

97. Ibid., 166.

98. Ibid.

99. Ibid., 165, n186.

100. Can Const. (Constitution Act, 1982) Pt. I (Canadian Charter of Rights & Freedoms).

101. Can Const. (Constitution Act, 1982) Pt. I (Canadian Charter of Rights & Freedoms) 15.

102. *Keegstra*, 3 S.C.R. at 756.

103. Brian M. Blugerman, "Beyond Obscenity: Canada's New Child Pornography Law," 11 *WTR Ent. & Sports Law* 3, 10 (Winter, 1994).

104. Brian M. Blugerman, "Beyond Obscenity: Canada's New Child Pornography Law," 11 *WTR Ent. & Sports Law* 3 (Winter, 1994).

105. Committee on Sexual Offenses against Children and Youth, *Sexual Offenses against Children: Report of the Committee on Sexual Offenses against Children,* Minister of Services Canada (Ottawa 1984); Special Committee on Pornography and Prostitution, *Pornography and Prostitution in Canada: Report of the Special Committee on Pornography and Prostitution,* Minister of Supply and Services Canada (Ottawa 1985).

106. N. Trocme, "Estimating the Scope of Child Abuse and Neglect in Ontario," *Research Connection* at 9 (Sept. 1993).

107. Code, ss. 151, 150.1.

108. Code, s. 153.

109. Code, s. 159; Brian M. Blugerman, "Beyond Obscenity: Canada's New Child Pornography Law," 11 *WTR Ent. & Sports Law* 3 n29 (Winter, 1994).

110. Mike McIntyre, "Judge Throws Out Child Porn Challenge," *Winnipeg Free Press*, (Feb. 3, 2000).

111. Hugh Potter, *Pornography: Group Pressures and Individual Rights,* (Sydney: Federation, 1996).

112. Kirsten Lawson, "PM to Revisit Porn-Video Rating Debate," *Canberra Times*, (March 8, 2000).

113. Barbara Sullivan, *The Politics of Sex: Prostitution and Pornography in Australia since 1945*, (New York: Cambridge University Press, 1997).

114. Ibid., 7.

115. Potter, *Pornography*, 53.

116. Sullivan, *Politics of Sex*, 32.

117. Ibid., 33.

118. *R. v. Hicklin*, 3 QB 360.

119. Sullivan, *Politics of Sex*, 33.

120. Ibid., 33–34.

121. Ibid., 38.

122. Ibid.

123. Marilyn Lake, "Female Desires: The Meaning of World War II," 24 *Australian Historical Studies* 95, 267 (1984).

124. Sullivan, *Politics of Sex*, 96.

125. Ibid., 89.

126. Ibid.

127. Lawson, "PM to Revisit Debate."

128. Ibid.

129. Johannes Nugroho, "Pornography: A Social Menace?" *Jakarta Post*, (July 15, 1999).

130. Potter, *Pornography*, 61.

131. Ibid.

132. Lawson, "PM to Revisit Debate."

133. Potter, *Pornography*, 53.

134. Ibid.

135. Ibid., 55.

136. Sullivan, *Politics of Sex*, 227.

137. Ibid., 51.

138. Ibid.

139. Ibid.

140. Ibid.

141. Ibid.

142. Ibid., 57.

143. Ibid.

144. Ibid.

145. Ibid., 52.

146. Ibid.

147. Ibid.

148. Ibid., 74.

149. Ibid., 73.

150. Nagroho, "Social Menace?"

151. Potter, *Pornography*, 132.

152. Ibid., 56.

153. Sullivan, *Politics of Sex*, 12.

154. Potter, *Pornography*, 68–69.

155. Sullivan, *Politics of Sex*, 68–69.

156. Ibid., 236.

157. Ibid., 230–31.

158. Ibid., 228–36.

159. Ibid., 236.

160. Lawson, "PM to Revisit Debate."

161. Sullivan, *Politics of Sex*, 236.

162. Ibid.

163. Ibid., 233–34.

164. Adam Creed, "Porn Site Evades Australian Censorship Laws," Newsbytes News Network (Feb. 3, 2000).

165. Shaun Anthony, "Alston to Tackle Porn on the Net," *West Australian*, (Mar. 20, 1999).

166. Potter, *Pornography*, 61.

167. Ibid.

168. Ibid., 78.

169. Ibid., 84.

170. Ibid., 132.

171. Ibid., 133.

172. Ibid., 134.

173. Ibid., 144.

174. Ibid., 149.

175. Ibid., 166.

176. Sullivan, *Politics of Sex*, 199.

177. Ibid., 2.

178. Ibid., 199–205.

179. Ibid., 235.

180. Anne B. Summers, *Damned Whores and God's Police: The Colonization of Women in Australia* (Ringwood: Penguin, 1975).

Chapter Two

Western Europe and Eastern Europe

WESTERN EUROPE

Europeans generally tolerate more explicit sex but less violence than Americans. For this survey, we found sufficient current information on England, Ireland, and Germany. Other nations, including Denmark, Sweden, West Germany, and the Netherlands were studied by Berl Kutchinsky,[1] who found that violent crime had not increased, and indeed in some cases had decreased, after the decriminalization of pornography in these European countries.

The Netherlands, Denmark, and Sweden do not regulate pornography. The Netherlands has the reputation as the most liberal country in Europe. While the open display of pornographic material has never been legal, hard-core pornography is readily available. Both the police and vendors ignore the law.[2] Denmark decriminalized the sex industry in the late 1960s. It allows its citizens unlimited access to pornography. As a result, sales of pornography initially jumped to an estimated 30 million pounds sterling in 1969; but by the end of 1970, the figure plummeted to around 12 million pounds, less than half of what it had been the previous year.[3] Sweden went one step further. It has no laws against child pornography. In 1994, the Swedish Parliament considered an amendment to the Swedish constitution that would make the possession of child pornography illegal, but the parliamentary constitutional committee established to study changes to the constitution voted against passage of the bill.[4] In a television interview granted by

Queen Silvia on July 23, 1996, she proposed that newspapers pub-
lish the names of convicted pedophiles rather than continue to protect their identities.

In regard to child pornography, laws differ throughout Europe.
For example, the possession of child pornography is illegal in
Britain, Germany, and Holland, but no such laws have been enacted
in Hungary, France, or Sweden.[5] Surprisingly, Holland has reportedly eliminated pornography on the Internet, and England and Germany are developing reporting systems to address the problem of illegal pornography on the Internet.[6] Even where there are laws
against pornography, they are often minimally utilized.

In Italy, for example, obscenity laws are vague. Child pornography is outlawed, but otherwise local judges decide what can go on
sale. This has led to extreme variations among local authorities. For
example, pornography is practically unobtainable in Brescia but
freely available in Milan.[7] Generally, however, Italians take a liberal
approach toward pornography.

The nations surveyed below tend to be more restrictive than the
rest of Europe. News and periodical reports on pornography are
largely limited to countries where pornography laws are in flux and
under pressure. Of course, current information is easier to find on
those nations where English is the native language. In dealing with
this severe limitation, it is important to recognize that Europe has
some of the most liberal laws toward pornography anywhere in the
world. Television stations regularly broadcast nudity, and, as already
mentioned, in some nations pornography is entirely unregulated. No
deleterious effects have been reported.

ENGLAND

Britain's obscenity laws are strict by European standards.[8] One television producer complained: "We are still not allowed to show pen-
etrative sex on television. Viewers cannot see an erect penis on television."[9] While these laws restrict the presentation of pornography,
the British population is still largely tolerant of sexual materials in
the media. X-rated theaters, adult bookstores, and massage parlors
are readily available in almost all communities, ranging from large

cities to small towns.[10] The British, however, do force filmmakers to cut violent scenes from movies.

The British Board of Film Classification can refuse a video certification on the grounds of sexual content. Under the Cinemas Act of 1985, local authorities must license any cinema in their area and approve the films shown. The Broadcasting Act of 1999 contains a provision on the importance of taste and decency on television and radio. At the same time, British juries are reluctant to convict unless the obscenity involves children, violence, or hard-core pornography.[11]

In England, unlike the United States, the protection of speech does not rest on fundamental constitutional grounds. It has instead developed through the common law and statutory provisions.[12] In *R. v. Hicklin*, Lord Cockburn defined the test for obscenity. Material is obscene if it has the tendency to deprave and corrupt those whose minds are open to immoral influences, and into whose hands these kinds of materials may fall.[13] Parliament incorporated this view into the Obscene Publications Act of 1959. As amended in 1965, this act is the law governing pornography in England and Wales. The test of whether the article is obscene is the same under the act as in common law except that the act requires the jury to look at the work as a whole, and at all the relevant circumstances, when assessing the material's likely effects on the reader.[14]

An article, therefore, is deemed obscene by its "effect." As provided in section 1(1), "an article shall be deemed to be obscene if its effect or (where the article comprises two or more distinct items) the effect of any one of its items is, if taken as a whole, such as to tend to deprave and corrupt persons who are likely, having regard to all relevant circumstances, to read, see or hear it."[15] To be convicted of the crime of obscenity, one must be found to possess an "obscene" article, which may be a film, book, video, or sculpture, etc., with a view to "publication of an obscene article for gain." Except for child pornography, mere possession is insufficient.[16] This includes the public display of indecent material and the supply and possession of unclassified material.[17] Section 1(3) defines "publication" as when a person "sells, lets or hires, gives or lends, distributes or circulates," including downloading obscene material from a computer or from satellite television.[18] The maximum penalty on

summary conviction is six months' imprisonment and, on indict-
ment, three years.[19]

The depravity to which the act refers is not confined to sex. Articles encouraging violence or drug abuse can be construed as obscene, too.[20] "To deprave" means to make morally bad or morally
worse; to pervert, to debase.[21] "To corrupt" means to render morally
unsound or rotten, to ruin a good quality, to defile, etc.[22] The purpose or intention of the distributor of the article is immaterial.[23] The
tendency to deprave and corrupt, however, must affect a significant
number of people in the society, not just a few "oddballs"; it must
affect more than a negligible handful of people.[24] In other words, the
act has adopted a relative conception of obscenity. An article cannot
be considered obscene in itself; it can only be so in relation to its
likely users. The key issue is the effect on the user's mind or emo-
tions rather than on behavior. Depravity and corruption are conditions of the mind, although "evidence of behavior may be necessary
to establish their presence."[25] The fact that a text encourages unlawful acts does not in itself render the material obscene. In practice,
judges tend to leave the determination to the jury.[26]

The act grants wide discretion to juries to determine the relevant
standard. The jury must decide who are the likely readers and
whether the material is likely to deprave and corrupt them.[27] In determining the effects of the material, the jury will not normally hear
expert evidence unless knowledge of the effects of the material is
likely to fall outside the bounds of the ordinary juror's experience.
British courts have interpreted the phrase so as to emphasize that the
effect of the sexual material must surpass the shocking, disgusting,
or immoral suggestion to constitute a serious menace to readers and
viewers.[28] Shock or disgust on the part of the jurors themselves is
insufficient to establish obscenity.[29] Rather, jurors are presumed to
be aware of the effects in most cases. This poses problems when
assessing likely harms, as it means that most of the social scientific
research on the impact of pornography would be excluded, even
though it is arguable whether this lies within the realm of common
sense rather than specialist knowledge. The presumption of the
harmlessness of pornography is a widely held view.[30] Once a decision has been reached on whether the material is obscene, the jury
must then consider various defenses allowed under the act.[31]

The primary defense is the "public good" defense. Section 4 states that:

> (1) A person shall not be convicted of an offence against section 2 of this Act . . . if it is proved that publication of the article in question is justified as being for the public good on the ground that it is in the interests of science, literature, art or learning, or of other objects of general concern. (2) It is hereby declared that the opinion of experts as to the literary, artistic, scientific or other merits of an article may be admitted in any proceedings under this Act either to establish or to negative the said ground.[32]

Expert evidence on the psychotherapeutic benefits of pornography, however, is inadmissible,[33] thereby excluding evidence on the cathartic effects of pornography in releasing sexual tensions or providing a harmless release for potential sexual offenders, although pornography has been used in psychiatric programs. While either side may submit expert evidence on the artistic or other merits under the public good defense in section 4(1), as we saw earlier, they may not present scientific evidence on the substantive issue of obscenity itself, which must normally be left to the jury.[34]

Ever since the futile 1976 prosecution of the exploitation paperback *Inside Linda Lovelace*, the Department of Public Prosecution has refrained from using the 1959 Obscenity Act against any written matter with the slightest pretense of literary or sociological merit.[35] Another, unrelated defense protects unwitting publishers and distributors from prosecution. Section 2(5) provides that an offense is not committed if the person can prove that he has not examined the article and had no cause to suspect that his publication of it would make him liable to be convicted.[36] Authorities often can avoid all of this by utilizing the forfeiture procedure under section 3 of the act. Section 3 permits prosecuting authorities to seize under warrant obscene material and take it to the nearest magistrate to be destroyed. These proceedings are preferred by police and prosecutors and are seldom challenged by defendants. Law enforcement prefers forfeiture because it's quick and avoids the uncertainties of a trial. Defendants prefer forfeiture to criminal proceedings, because while they may lose their stock, they won't lose their businesses.

The Obscene Publication Act also punishes the showing and distribution of unclassified films. Films shown in British cinemas are subject to at least four types of government regulation: (1) prosecution under the 1959 Obscene Publications Act; (2) certification by the British Board of Film Classification (BBFC); (3) refusal by a local council under the Local Government (Miscellaneous Provisions) Act (1982) to accept BBFC classifications, which in particular cases could mean denial of an exhibition license to show the film in cinemas within the council's jurisdiction; and (4) authority granted to customs officials to refuse entry into the country to any film considered "indecent."[37] The 1981 Indecent Displays (Control) Act created a new statutory offense prohibiting the display of indecent matter visible from a public place or displayed in a place, such as a store, to which the public has access. The act includes materials from magazine covers to cinema posters but excludes displays which the public must pay to see or which the public can enter only after passing a prescribed warning notice and to which persons under eighteen are not admitted.

Film regulation in Britain rests on the power of local governments to issue licenses to commercial businesses such as pubs and music halls. Every film and videotape distributed in Britain is subject to the BBFC.[38] The prescribed ratings include: U, Universal, suitable for all ages; PG, Parental Guidance, includes some scenes unsuitable for young children; 12, suitable for children over twelve years old, the age where they are just out of the primary grades; 15, suitable for children over fifteen years old, in the last year of compulsory schooling; 18, suitable for persons over eighteen years old; and R-18, restricted to adults only and available only in specially licensed cinemas or sex shops to which no person under eighteen is admitted. The BBFC always considers the likely audience for a particular work. For example, art-house movies, particularly if they are subtitled, do have a restricted circulation.[39] The BBCF's ratings are, however, strictly enforced at local theaters.[40] Decisions of the BBFC may be appealed.[41]

The general purpose of the 1984 Video Recording Act is to regulate the distribution of video recordings in Britain, with exemptions for video games and videos produced to inform, educate, or instruct and those concerned with sports, music, or religion. Section 2(2) of the act applies to videos that depict:

a. human sexual activity or acts of force or restraint associated with such activity
b. mutilation or torture of, or other acts of gross violence towards, humans or animals
c. human genital organs or human urinary or excretory functions

The act empowered the secretary of state to select an authority with responsibility for reviewing videotapes and determining their suitability for being viewed in the home. The secretary assigned that task to the BBFC, which then began to examine videos in the same way it examines cinema films except that it set standards for certification that were stricter than for films because videos would enter the home. Videos found unsuitable for classification are denied certificates, while adult-type videos are assigned to licensed sex shops where they are available only to persons over eighteen.[42] To supply uncertified videos or to rent or sell videos in breach of the classification assigned is an offense subject to a penalty up to 20,000 pounds.[43] The BBFC had succeeded at least in ridding Britain of its most offensive videos.

Recognizing that VCRs provide the capability to focus in on, repeat, and freeze-frame the more sexually explicit and violent scenes, the 1984 Video Recording Act grants the BBFC the authority to require the tape version of a film to adhere to a higher standard of audience suitability since it will be viewed at home rather than in a public theater.[44] For example, while *I Spit on Your Grave, House on the Side of the Park*, and *Faces of Death* are available for rental to children in the United States without an MPAA classification or rating, the British ruled these videos legally obscene and banned them from the country.[45] The classification of videos in the UK also leads to many more cuts and rejections than for films released for cinema viewing. The Academy Award–winning film *The Silence of the Lambs* was granted an 18 certificate for showing in cinemas, but when the film was released on video, the BBFC insisted on several cuts to tone down the violence before it would agree to the 18 rating. Furthermore, the BBFC is not hesitant to ban some videos altogether.

This is what happened when the board banned *Bad Lieutenant, Dirty Weekend,* and *Reservoir Dogs,* preventing their release on videotape. In this sense, the British system operates on a double standard, one for cinema films, another for videos. It justifies the distinction on the grounds that British youngsters under eighteen who were not permitted to see movies like *The Silence of the Lambs* in the cinema would be able to see the video version at home or at a friend's house without parental knowledge. Americans might consider this system overly paternalistic, but the British do not seem to mind.

British Public Opinion

A homogeneous population and a paternalistic ethos provide support for government regulation of personal and public morality in Britain.[46] The Williams Committee, a 1979 committee commissioned by the British government to study the issue of pornography, concluded that the thrust of British policy toward pornography should be restrictive rather than prohibitive and that a regulatory policy should be directed toward protecting children and shielding such material from the segment of the population that finds it offensive.[47] Parents in Britain do not seem offended by the BBFC's apparent preemption of parental responsibility, possibly because logic dictates that the mere presence of an adult with a child does not automatically convert the content of an 18-rated film into PG.[48] Still, recent studies indicate that British children are often exposed to pornography.

More than half of the youngsters polled in a recent survey were able to see films on videos that were classified unsuitable for their age category.[49] Forty-five percent of British schoolchildren between the ages of seven and sixteen had seen at least one banned video, while 22 percent had seen four or more. Fifty-seven percent had viewed at least one R-18 film. Beyond this, the British are generally happy with their system.

According to a poll commissioned by the 1999 Edinburgh Television Festival, of the 1,868 people questioned, 64 percent said that they were happy with the amount of sex on television, provided that sex scenes were not "tacky or grubby."[50] Meanwhile, the Independent Television Commission found that less than a third of viewers reported they had seen or heard anything offensive on television, the lowest proportion since the survey began.[51] The main causes of offense were bad language, followed by violence and then sex. Meanwhile, the Broadcasting Standards Commission's annual *Monitoring Report* showed that, when asked whether violence, bad language or sex on television caused them most concern, 58 percent cited violence, 24 percent bad language, and 12 percent sex. Asked if the amount of sex on television was too much, about right, or too little, 38 percent said too much, a response that has remained little changed from previous surveys.[52] The year's most comprehensive surveys of sexuality on television, the Broadcasting Standards Commission's *Sex and Sensibility* study, similarly found that 36 percent of respondents said that there was too much sex on television.[53] Some 78 percent of all respondents thought that sexual activity should be depicted if part of a story line, but 72 percent felt that sex was being used to increase ratings.

Child Pornography

There is, however, growing intolerance for explicit violence and child pornography. One author reported that there is a strong popular belief in Britain that what you see on the screen can influence subsequent behavior, particularly in regard to violence.[54] This intolerance is also evident in new laws against child pornography. It is an offense for a person: (a) to take, or permit to be taken, or to make any indecent photograph or pseudophotograph of a child. The Protection of Children Act of 1978 is similar to the Obscene Publications Act, except that the material must only meet a standard of indecency rather than obscenity.[55] By UK standards, a photo that is not obscene may still be indecent. Furthermore, a photo that may not even be considered indecent when depicting an adult may be indecent if a child is involved. The Criminal Justice Act of 1988 makes it a crime to possess an indecent photograph of a child,[56] and the Criminal Justice and Public Order Act of 1994 amended the Protection of Children Act 1978 to make downloading and/or printing out of computer data of indecent images of children an offense.[57] Unlike the obscenity laws, mere possession of child pornography is sufficient to constitute an offense.[58]

IRELAND

Ireland offers the strictest pornography legislation in Western Europe.[59] After decades of censorship, and amid some protest, Ireland legalized *Playboy* in 1995.[60] Ireland's prohibition on divorce remained in place until 1995.[61] Ireland prohibited information on contraception until 1979, and only a 1992 referendum on abortion allowed access to abortion information.[62]

At the same time, however, only films destined to be exhibited to the general public are submitted to the censor. Films exhibited in private clubs where admission is substantially restricted, such as film festivals, student film societies, and art houses, evade censorship. And even films available to the general public are rarely cut.[63] Also widely available are British broadcast television programs which display rather explicit sexual material. Additionally, newspapers called "dailies," which report on sexual scandals and include ubiquitous pictures of topless models, thrive in Ireland.

The recent concession to *Playboy*, however, has not signaled a general retreat on the prohibition of pornography. Pornographic magazines and videos are often banned. All the while, Ireland's marketplace of ideas thrives notwithstanding the censorship of pornography.[64]

Irish Legal Approaches

Ireland's constitution establishes a parliamentary democracy, presupposes a homogeneous Catholic culture, evokes the greater goal of social equality by establishing limits on the use of private property,[65] and explicitly establishes education and family rights.[66] For example, the Irish guarantee of free expression is explicitly qualified, not once, but twice. First, this guarantee is made "subject to public order and morality."[67] It is limited by this provision:

> The education of public opinion being, however, a matter of such grave import to the common good, the State shall endeavor to ensure that organs of public opinion, such as the radio, the press, the cinema, while preserving their rightful liberty of expression, including criticism of Government policy, shall not be used to undermine public order or morality or the authority of the State. The publication or utter-

ance of blasphemous, seditious, or indecent matter is an offence which shall be punishable in accordance with law.[68]

This bald restriction on free speech in Ireland might surprise some American observers. But in some respects the limits posed by "public order, or morality or the authority of the State"[69] parallel exceptions to the First Amendment's guarantee of free speech created by the U.S. Supreme Court's concern about public order and morality evident in the fighting words, obscenity, and "clear and present danger" exceptions to the First Amendment.

The Censorship of Publications Act of 1929 established four criminal offenses based on the following materials: prohibited books and periodicals; indecent pictures; material that promotes abortion or contraception; and certain materials related to judicial proceedings. Material is indecent if it is "suggestive of, or inciting to sexual immorality or unnatural vice or likely in any other similar way to corrupt or deprave."[70] One can be punished for importing, offering for sale, or publishing indecent pictures.[71] While the term "obscene" is used, no definition is offered for it. Finally, periodicals alone may be prohibited if they devote an unduly large proportion of space to the publication of matter relating to crime.[72]

Banning a book or periodical is alarmingly simple: a member of the public or a customs official can submit the material to the board for review.[73] The board has the authority to issue a prohibition order which, originally, only the minister of justice could revoke.

Until 1946, there was no appeals process. Until 1967 there was no time limit on the effect of a prohibition order. After 1967, a time limit of twelve years applied to every order. One significant mitigating provision applies only to books. When considering prohibition of a book, the board considers the book's literary, artistic, scientific, or historic merit; its general tenor; the language in which the book is printed; its intended circulation; the class of its reader; and any other relevant matter.[74] Books banned by the board in the past include Hemingway's *A Farewell to Arms*, Huxley's *Brave New World*, Joyce's *Stephen Hero*, Mead's *Coming of Age in Samoa*, Steinbeck's *The Grapes of Wrath*, and Beckett's *Watt*.[75] There has, however, been a radical change of emphasis in the criteria used by the board. Now the board bans few literary works and instead focuses on sex magazines, films, and videos.[76]

Films are governed by the Censorship of Films Act of 1923. Films must be approved by the official censor, who may refuse a certificate if he believes the film to be "unfit by reason of being indecent, obscene or blasphemous."[77] Only eleven films have been cut in the last eight years. The censor can also ban a video which would tend to "deprave or corrupt persons who might view it."[78]

The 1989 Video Recordings Act (VRA) provides that:

Section 3(1) The Official censor shall, on application to him in relation to a video work, grant to the person making the application (referred to in this section as the applicant) a certificate (referred to in this Act as a supply certificate) declaring the work to be fit for viewing unless he is of opinion that the work is unfit for viewing because

(a) the viewing of it—
  (i) would be likely to cause persons to commit crimes, whether by inciting or encouraging them to do so or by indicating or suggesting ways of doing so or of avoiding detection, or
  (ii) would tend, by reason of the inclusion in it of obscene or indecent matter, to deprave or corrupt a person who might view it,
(b) it depicts acts of gross violence or cruelty (including mutilation or torture) towards humans or animals.[79]

A certificate for public exhibition is required, and that certificate can only be issued by the censor. The censor has the power to issue certificates for exhibition to certain classes of audiences (e.g., "under 12 must be accompanied by an adult"). The censor also has power to deny a certificate. Finally, in the case of films, distributors have been willing to make cuts as requested by the censor in order to receive a certificate. In the case of videos, the VRA does not permit that compromise.

Under the VRA it is an offense to possess in order to supply, or to offer to supply, a video that is either uncertified or prohibited. It is also an offense to display for the public an uncertified or prohibited video.[80] To complete the regulatory scheme, a licensing system is established for video retailers and video rental companies. Finally, it is an offense to import a prohibited video. A random survey of twenty titles from the list of 1994 prohibition orders found that 50 percent had obviously pornographic titles.[81]

Number of Video Prohibition Orders Issued 1991–1997[82]

1991	1992	1993	1994	1995	1996	1997*
34	253	304	931	407	527	58

*January to July only.

This indicates that over 95 percent of material banned is pornographic. Following the example set in prior legislation, mere possession is not criminalized.

GERMANY

While Germany is more restrictive than other Western European countries, pornography is available in Germany. The print media in Germany is largely unrestricted. Pornography is forbidden on television, but hard-core pornographic movies can be rented from video stores or ordered on a pay-per-view basis in German hotels.[83] Germany is considered a major producer of child pornography, though child pornography is illegal in Germany.[84] Germany recently made moves to address the problem of illegal pornography on the Internet.[85] Germany's more restrictive approach is at least partly the result of its history. Germans are concerned about Nazi hate speech, and so their new laws also prohibit hate speech.

Germany takes a slightly more restrictive approach to freedom of speech, because of its history. Nazi propaganda successfully radicalized the German people prior to World War II, and there is some fear that if left unchecked, Nazi propaganda or other hate speech could seriously threaten the peace again. This restriction, however, has been carefully balanced to ensure freedom of the press and opinion while restricting and even eliminating threatening hate speech.

Legal Approaches

The German press is basically free from state interference. The press is privately owned, and there is no licensing, censorship, or state involvement in the editorial process. Since 1961, the Constitutional

Court has viewed the freedom of broadcast as a freedom in service of the people and democracy. Specifically because the broadcast media affect opinion formation, the Constitutional Court has concluded that the basic values protected by the freedom of broadcast clause constitutionally necessitate legislative action. The German Constitutional Court has expressly required the legislature to pass laws that are supposed to guarantee quality, objectivity, diversity, and the furtherance of democratic values.[86] Article 5 of the German Basic Law states:

(1) Each person has the right freely to express and disseminate his opinion in word, writing, and picture, and to obtain information from generally accessible sources without interference. The freedom of the press and the freedom to report information through broadcast and film are guaranteed. There shall be no censorship.
(2) These rights are limited by the provisions of the general laws, the laws for the protection of minors, and the law of personal honor.
(3) Art, science, research, and teaching are free. Freedom of teaching does not absolve from fidelity to the constitution.[87]

The German Basic Law demands legislation regulating private broadcasting. Such legislation must provide the conditions necessary to guarantee the freedom of broadcast. In order to be effective, the freedom of broadcast must be legislatively supported. This necessity results from the purpose and the special character of the constitutional guarantee at issue. The freedom of broadcast serves the same purpose as all guarantees of article 5.1 of the Basic Law: "to ensure the formation of free individual and public opinion in a comprehensive way that includes every transmission of information and opinion and is not limited to the mere reporting of news or to the transmission of political opinions." A free formation of opinion takes place in a process of communication. It is predicated, on the one hand, on the freedom to express and disseminate opinions and, on the other, on the freedom to take notice of expressed opinions and to inform oneself.

In its *Mephisto* opinion of 1971, for example, the court affirmed a lower court's prohibition of the publication of Klaus Mann's novel *Mephisto*. In the novel, Mann portrays Gustaf Grundgens as an "abject type of the treacherous intellectual who prostitutes his talent for the sake of some tawdry fame and transitory wealth" during the Third Reich. Grundgens's stepson sued the publisher of the novel, reasoning that the portrayal violated his (deceased) father's human dignity, which is protected by article 1 of the Basic Law. The court held that freedom of art, expressly granted in article 5.3, may have to yield to human dignity concerns despite the fact that the rights protected by article 5.3 are formulated in an absolute fashion. Reasoning that freedom of art is not an autonomous freedom but rather part of the constitutional value system and ultimately an emanation from article 1's guarantee of human dignity, the court stated:

> [Freedom of art] is not granted without limitations. Like all basic rights, [freedom of art] is based on the Basic Law's image of the human being, i.e., based on the human being as an independent and responsible personality who freely unfolds within the social community. . . . [A] conflict that arises with respect to the freedom of art must be solved through constitutional interpretation according to the value order of the Basic Law and according to the unity of this fundamental value system. As part of the Basic Law's system of values, freedom of art is particularly associated with the dignity of the human being guaranteed in Art. 1, which as supreme value dominates the entire value system of the Basic Law. . . . Despite that [association], freedom of art can conflict with the similarly constitutionally protected personal sphere because a work of art can have consequences on a social level.[88]

The court, therefore, balanced the violation of the personal sphere of the plaintiff against the speech rights of the defendant and upheld the lower court's ruling that the dignity interest of Mr. Grundgens, the deceased, outweighed the interest protected by the freedom of art.

Freedom of broadcast became a subordinate interest in the service of a greater good, namely, helping the public to form opinions. The supreme court argued that freedom of broadcast serves the purpose of opinion formation. Dismissing the libertarian approach, the court held that the Basic Law required legislative supervision of broadcast:

> Thus what is needed is a positive order that ensures that the multiplicity of existing opinions is expressed through broadcast in the

greatest possible breadth and completeness, and that thereby comprehensive information is offered. In order to accomplish this, substantive, organizational and procedural regulations are necessary that
are designed according to the task of the freedom of broadcast and
are therefore able to accomplish that which Article 5.1 of the Basic
Law is supposed to guarantee.[89]

This balanced approach has not led to a wholesale ban on pornography or on "high-value" speech, such as political, artistic, literary, or
scientific speech, though Nazi hate speech is banned, as is child
pornography.

Child Pornography

The Child Commission of the German Bundestag has proposed legislation that addresses the distribution of child pornography on the Internet. The commission's goals are to promote rapid coordination of
international law, regulate the mandatory storage of Internet service
provider records for criminal prosecution purposes, and amend section
184 of the German criminal code to make computer-generated child
pornography a criminal offense. The commission has recommended a
two-pronged approach to eliminating child pornography on the Internet. First, it would create the German Internet Content Task Force. The
task force would block Germans' access to prohibited material and
newsgroups. Secondly, the task force would lend technical support to
German law enforcement agencies who would prosecute violations.

CONCLUSION (WESTERN EUROPE)

Western Europe is liberal in its approach to pornography. The trend,
however, is toward more restrictions. This is probably because there
is no place else to go following complete deregulation. It does not
appear that complete deregulation will sweep Europe anytime soon.
Most countries are working toward a balance between individual
rights and community concerns. Even though complete deregulation
has not led to any deleterious effects, nations do not wish to promote
a policy to which their people may be opposed. A certain degree of
regulation may make people feel better, but it is unclear whether it

affects women's and children's well-being. But perhaps feeling better is a justifiable result. People want freedom, but they also want to live in what they perceive to be a good society. In Europe, while the trend appears to be toward more regulation, it is not a strong trend and will probably be limited in its extent.

EASTERN EUROPE

The fall of communism released a flood of pornography on many countries in Eastern Europe. In some cases, organized crime has taken over, thus leading to a wave of child and violent pornography. Some countries already had laws allowing sex with teenagers. In Hungary, for example, soliciting sex with a fifteen-year-old is legal.[90] Many of the nations are trying to reconcile the new freedoms of democracy with the old law-and-order values of authoritarianism. Many of the older people are more comfortable with the old values, while the young revel in their new freedoms.

RUSSIA

Pornography is abundant in postcommunist Russia. Market pressures, after the fall of Communism, encouraged the spread of pornography.[91] Naked bodies adorn mainstream journals and newspapers. Domestic and imported movies regularly feature sex scenes. Television portrays explicit sex during regular prime time hours.[92] Pirated foreign pornographic videos were reported in large numbers as early as 1988. Previously confiscated at the border, pornographic literature now comes in freely from Sweden, Denmark, the Netherlands, Germany, and the United States.[93] Initially, local pornography had not been as explicit as Western pornography, but that was only because the producers had not yet matched the "standards" of Western pornographers. Russian pornography, like its Western counterpart, is evolving toward more and more degrading sex involving violence and pedophilia.[94]

Underage prostitution and child pornography are growing in Russia. In Moscow alone, an estimated one thousand girls under eighteen are involved in prostitution. The youngest, colloquially called "whores with hair ribbons" or "junior" prostitutes, are as young as six years old. Most are runaways or were abducted or "purchased" from their parents. There is a close tie between these prostitutes and the child pornography industry. Pornographic films involving both "junior" and "senior" juveniles have been in increasing demand. The younger girls are normally shown in ordinary pornographic scenes, having sex with a man or woman; but the older girls are often depicted engaging in various types of fetishes. Videocassettes with scenes showing twelve to fifteen-year-old girls urinating and defecating or having sex with dogs are currently circulating in Moscow.[95]

Russian Legal Approaches

There are obscenity statutes on the books, but the laws simply go unenforced. Although the lack of enforcement can be attributed to a matter of priorities, part of the problem is the Russian government's difficulty in defining the limits of democratic freedom and the meaning of democracy itself.[96] "Glasnost" is often erroneously translated in the West as "openness." Westerners interpreted it as "freedom of speech." The word's meaning, however, is much more subtle. "Glasnost" really means "publicity." Its root is *glas/golos*, meaning "voice." The word glasnost then literally means "voiceness," or the articulation of voices. Mikhail Gorbachev meant it as a virtual national suggestion box. The grassroots would articulate their needs and criticisms to higher authorities. The authorities would respond to and solve these problems for the people. Gorbachev intended these many voices to support his political reform by bypassing the stagnant Brezhnev-era bureaucracy and not challenging him directly. Yeltsin's attitude toward mass participation was not all that different. He wanted the people's ideas to support the decisions he made.[97] Freedom of speech as we envision it in the West does not truly exist in Russia yet, but there continues to be slow progress toward greater liberty.

Pornography is also understood differently in Russia. Contemporary conservatives in Russia tend to support the notion that pornography is one of a series of symptoms of a society that has forgotten its moral values. The social disruption occurring now, they attest, is caused not by political upheaval but by seventy years of atheism and a lack of strong authority in society. Conservative politicians appeal to disillusioned Russians with promises to eradicate pornography and "the cult of violence." The debate is colored by a society that is traditional, perhaps even premodern, yet buffeted by postmodern cultural images and thought.[98]

Conservatives have usually dominated the debate in Russia. Russians have no strong experience with freedom of the press. They have a much wider experience with censorship and the idea that the media are servants of the state. These ideas fit much better with conservative solutions to pornography. Censorship and elite control over culture are understood. Nineteenth-century English liberalism is still in its infancy in Russia.[99]

Russian obscenity laws, from the czarist era to the present, stresses the distribution of pornography as an actionable offense.[100] During the Soviet era, this reflected a Marxist-Leninist interest in controlling the market in pornography. The charge had to be phrased in the language of market relations and economic exploitation. The accused could not be attacked for corrupting his own morality but only for economically exploiting others.[101] This approach remains in effect today.

On June 12, 1990, Gorbachev passed a press law promising to safeguard freedom of speech and ban censorship *except* in regard to divulging state secrets or secrets specifically protected by the law; advocating the forcible overthrow of the state or forcible change of the existing social system; promoting war, violence, or brutality; inciting racial, national, or religious exclusivity or intolerance; or disseminating pornography or other materials with a view to the commission of other criminally punishable acts not allowed.[102] As a result, some periodic attempts have been made to stem the spread of pornography. Moscow city authorities adopted proclamations to ban the sale of pornography but took little action. Consumers still have little trouble getting pornography. Newsstand operators set out open attaché cases full of German pornographic magazines. When law enforcement officers appear, the dealers quickly close the cases and push them under their tables. In a society traditionally known for its lack of consumer goods, it is significant that a recent survey indicated that Muscovite men own 50 percent more pornographic videotapes then their counterparts in London and 20 percent more than the average American male.[103]

At the end of 1991, Yeltsin promulgated his own press law. Unlike Gorbachev's law, this one specifically addressed the issue of "erotic publications." Erotic publications were only to be sold in special packaging and from special locations to be determined by local administrators. Furthermore, erotic radio and television broadcasts were limited to late-night hours. The law, however, has not been seriously enforced.[104]

On June 13, 1996, former president Boris Yeltsin signed into law a new criminal code for the Russian Federation, which took effect on January 1, 1997. Article 242 made it unlawful to circulate, distribute, advertise, or produce, with the goal of distribution, pornographic materials. Violators could be fined between 500 and 800 times the minimum wage, the earned wages of five to eight months, or imprisoned for up to two years.[105] Without any guidelines, however, article 242 actually legalized all pornography.[106]

Article 242 did not define pornography. Instead, commentary on the criminal code written in 1960 defined pornographic works as "rudely naturalistic, obscene, cynical portrayals of sexual life that attempt as their goal the unhealthy stimulation of sexual feelings."[107] This legal definition of pornography dominated the official commentaries through the late eighties and has survived to today as the authoritative guide to the Russian criminal justice approaches to regulating pornography.[108]

The Russian legal system encourages the use of "expert commissions" in court proceedings.[109] The average judge or the average person is considered unqualified to determine what is pornographic and what is erotic. The "expert" is trained in these matters. For example, a commissioner may have training as an art historian. These expert commissions created detailed guidelines for identifying pornographic videos. These guidelines have been modified for use in analyzing texts and still photographs as well. To analyze a film, the committee examines the structure and construction of each frame. The first criterion is to determine the artist's intent and focus. Does he concentrate on the physical part of sex or on an emotional or psychological part? Are the sex scenes relevant to the characters and the plot, or are they only there to portray sex? This criterion is an attempt to apply the "rudely naturalistic" language of the 1960 definition of pornography. The sex must further the story. It cannot be simply displayed in all its detail.[110] There are several other criteria that could be used to identify the intent of the filmmaker:

1. "Autoattribution": does the film identify itself as pornographic? (For example, is the film labled "XXX"?)
2. Anonymity: is a list of credits absent, or do the credits include a heavy use of pseudonyms?
3. Is the intentional portrayal of sexual scenes without artistic pretensions?
   a. Is a majority of the time in the film spent showing copulation?
   b. Does the film lack "artistic principles of construction" (i.e., an introduction, development, and conclusion)?
   c. Does the film lack plot or context?
   d. Is there continuity?
   e. Do the scenes merely repeat each other?
   f. Do the characters have any meaning outside of being representatives of their sex?
   g. Is the film edited to highlight the sex scenes?[111]

Physiological details and fetishism, such as group sex, bestiality, or exhibitionism, are good signs of pornography but are not conclusive in themselves. The work, however, must show naked genitals in order to be pornographic. Otherwise, the work may be offensive to taste but cannot be judged "pornographic" by legal standards.[112]

Russian Public Opinion

While some efforts have been made by the legislature to identify pornography as a civil offense, subject to civil, rather than criminal, penalties,[113] sexual representations have gained acceptability. As early as the mid-1970s, surveys revealed a wide acceptance of premarital sex, particularly in the large cities. One study showed that 71 percent of urban teenagers approved of premarital sex whereas only 54 percent of teenagers from the countryside did. Twenty-four percent of the rural respondents rejected premarital sex while 21 percent had given the question no thought at all, a response which the researchers felt indicated an even stronger conservative response than a simple rejection.[114] The same proved true for young Russians' attitudes toward pornography. A 1991 survey of fourteen hundred young people showed that 60 percent of them had seen a pornographic video at least once. Respondents who had grown up in urban areas were even more likely to have had such an experience, with almost 80 percent of them responding affirmatively.[115]

By 1993, public acceptance of pornography was quite high. Only 31 percent condemned it as unacceptable compared to 71 percent who condemned homosexuality and 47 percent who condemned masturbation.[116] Of the "controversial" sexual behaviors examined by the researchers, only premarital sex was less unacceptable (27 percent). While older respondents were more likely to condemn pornography than young ones, and young men were more likely to disapprove of pornography than young women, overall pornography remained acceptable relative to other issues.

At the same time, there are indications that many Russians believe their nation is in a state of moral decline. One survey showed that a large number of soldiers felt there was a moral decline going on in their society. Only 11 percent, however, attributed it to pornography. Still, 29 percent felt that pornography should be banned outright.[117]

While most Russian adults were concerned about keeping pornography out of the hands of children, they were not so worried about the use of pornography by adults. Over three-quarters of the total surveyed felt that regardless of any other controls there should be special sex shops where pornographic materials could be purchased by mature adults. Another survey found that 22 percent of European Russians read pornography. The figure placed Russia second only to Estonia for pornography consumption within the Soviet successor states.[118] Age breakdowns showed that the bulk of the conservative responses came from the elderly and from communists.[119]

Russians' interest in pornography has declined but remains significant. Sales of pornography dropped off by 1994. The venerable *SPID-Info,* Russia's sex-education magazine, suffered a decline in circulation but still sells an impressive figure of 4 million copies annually. Pornography has found a sizable niche market. Western-owned publications still dominate. *Playboy*'s Russian-language edition boasts a circulation of one hundred thousand. Pornography on the Internet has also belatedly made an appearance. While few Russians own personal computers, hundreds of "adult" websites have begun to proliferate.[120] In spite of the rhetoric, pornography remains widely available in Russia and includes a sizable black market.

POLAND

Pornography flourishes in sex shops and newsstands in post-communist Poland, a deeply and predominantly Catholic society.[121] Economic liberalization and lighter border controls following communism's collapse in 1989 opened the way for an influx of glossy European sex magazines and the growth of a domestic sex industry.[122] Indeed, the penal code that became effective in September 1998 effectively made pornography legal. Only qualified (or hard-core) pornography, such as that involving children, animals, and violence, as well as that imposed upon a person against his or her wish, remained an offense under the code.[123] These new laws may not stand. In December 1999 and early 2000, both houses of the Polish parliament passed legislation outlawing pornography and imposing lengthier prison sentences and fines. The offenders would face from one to ten years in prison instead of from three months to five years.[124]

In December of 1999, the Sejm, the Polish parliament's lower chamber, voted 233–156, with 12 abstentions, to increase top prison terms to two years from the current one year for dissemination of obscene material.[125] The measure doubles the maximum sentence for production and distribution of child or hard-core pornography to ten years and amends the definition of hard-core pornography to include content that shows sex organs during intercourse, effectively banning hard-core pornography.[126] The penalties apply to those convicted of dissemination of pornography in public or in a manner that forces it upon people against their will. It also prohibits distribution to minors and bans material dealing with pedophilia, sodomy, and necrophilia. Soft-core pornography can still be disseminated in Poland on condition that magazines carrying such content are wrapped so that their covers are not exposed. If these conditions are not met, the offender faces from three months to two years in prison.[127]

The Polish Senate Legal Affairs Committee proposed that the graphic depiction of sexual organs during intercourse should not be included under the definition, but leftists in the senate ultimately failed to amend the Solidarity-backed legislation.[128] Instead, by a majority of one vote, the senate on January 15, 2000, approved a complete ban on pornography, amending the act passed recently by the Sejm by not only banning hard-core pornography but also proposing a two-year sentence and an extra fine for producing and publishing pornography for profit.[129] The measure effectively eliminated the distinction between illegal hard-core and legal soft-core porn, thereby criminalizing all pornography.[130] The production and public sale of child pornography and hard-core material would be punishable by up to five years in prison. It was unclear whether the stringent measures would survive when the bill returned to the lower house, or whether President Aleksander Kwasniewski would approve the bill.[131] Debate on the amendments was stormy, with left-wing opposition questioning the wisdom of its introduction. Also some Freedom Union party members were against the changes. The move was strongly advocated by the ruling AWS Solidarity Election Action Party and members of the PSL Polish Peasant Party.[132]

As of the time of this writing, the Polish president had not yet signed the new legislation into law. The law on pornography in Poland, therefore, is still in flux and may change in the immediate future. A national poll conducted in January 2000 found that 78 percent of Poles think adults should have the right to watch naked girls in film or pictures and 56 percent had no objection to the sale of soft porn.

CONCLUSION (EASTERN EUROPE)

Those nations emerging from the depths of communism must now determine for themselves how they wish to cope with pornography. Each nation will draw on its own history to determine the level of freedom appropriate for its culture. This survey may be of use to these new countries. They can see how other nations deal with pornography and obscenity. No one way is the right way. By European standards, violent media should be more rigorously curtailed than mere sexual explicitness. A Catholic nation like Poland, however, may choose to follow a more restrictive approach similar to Ireland's. On the other hand, with the amount and type of pornography available and produced in Russia and Poland, an initial focus on the worst of it may be the chosen course of action.

NOTES

1. Berl Kutchinsky, *Experiences with Pornography and Prostitution in Denmark* (Copenhagen: Kriminalistisk institut, 1985); Berl Kutchinsky, "Pornography and Rape: Theory and Practice? Evidence for Crime Data in Four Countries Where Pornography Is Easily Available," 14 *Int'l J. of L. and Psychiatry* 47 (1991).

2. "Controlling Pornography: Law/How Britain Compares with Other Countries in Dealing with the Problem of Obscenity," *Guardian* (Aug. 13, 1998).

3. Johannes Nugroho, "Pornography: A Social Menace?" *Jakarta Post*, (July 15, 1999).

4. Jennifer Stewart, "If This Is the Global Community, We Must Be on the Bad Side of Town: International Policing of Child Pornography on the Internet," 20 *Hous. J. Int'l L.* 205, 222–23 (Fall 1997).

5. Ibid., 239.

6. Ibid., 232.

7. Ibid., 112.

8. Ibid.

9. Julian Petley, "Sex and Censure," 29 *Index on Censorship* 192, 194 (Jan. 2000).

10. Giglio, *Rights*, 111.

11. Ibid., 157.

12. Susan M. Easton, *The Problem of Pornography: Regulation and the Right to Free Speech* (New York: Routledge, 1994).

13. *R. v. Hicklin*, LR 3Qb 360 (1868).

14. Easton, *Problem of Pornography*, 125.

15. Ibid.

16. Ibid.

17. Susan S. M. Edwards, "On the Contemporary Application of the Obscene Publications Act" *1959*, 14 *Crim. R.* 843 (1998).

18. Ibid., 844–45.

19. Ibid.

20. Easton, *Problem of Pornography*, 126.

21. Edwards, "Contemporary Application," 849.

22. Ibid.

23. Ibid.

24. Ibid., 850.

25. *D.P.P. v. Whyte* AC 849, 871 (1972).

26. Edwards, "Contemporary Application," 850.

27. *D.P.P. v. Whyte* AC 849, 850 (1972).

28. Giglio, *Rights*, 157.

29. Easton, *Problem of Pornography*, 127.

30. *D.P.P. v. Whyte* AC 849, 850 (1972).

31. Easton, *Problem of Pornography*, 129.

32. *Director of Public Prosecutions v. Jordan*, 1976 WL 46168 (HL).

33. *D.P.P. v. Jordan* AC 699 (1977).

34. Easton, *Problem of Pornography*, 129.

35. Giglio, *Rights*, 157–58; Easton, *Problem of Pornography*, 125.

36. Easton, *Problem of Pornography*, 126.

37. Giglio, *Rights*, 162.

38. Ibid., 114–15.

39. Andreas Whittam Smith, "Porn, Violence, and What the Public Wants," *Independent*, (Nov. 8, 1999).

40. Giglio, *Rights*, 118.

41. Ibid., 115–16.

42. Ibid., 163–64.

43. Ibid.

44. Ibid., 129.

45. Ibid., 130.

46. Ibid., 164.

47. Ibid., 159.

48. Ibid., 135.

49. Ibid., 136.

50. Julian Petley, "Sex and Censure," 29 *Index on Censorship* 192, 193 (Jan. 2000).

51. Ibid.

52. Ibid.

53. Ibid., 193–94.

54. Andreas Whittam Smith, "Porn, Violence, and What the Public Wants," *Independent* (Nov. 8, 1999).

55. Dawn A. Edick, "Regulation of the Internet in the United States and the United Kingdom: A Comparative Analysis," 21 *B.C. Int'l & Comp. L. Rev.* 437 (Summer 1998).

56. Criminal Justice Act, 1988, ch. 33, 160 (Eng.).

57. "Friday Law Report: Downloading Internet Pornography an Offence," *Independent–London* (Nov. 26, 1999).

58. Easton, *Problem of Pornography.*

59. "Controlling Pornography; Law/How Britain Compares with Other Countries in Dealing with the Problem of Obscenity," *Guardian* (Aug. 13, 1998).

60. O'Callaghan, "Censorship of Indecency," 62.

61. Ibid., 57.

62. Ibid., 63, n57.

63. Ibid., 72.

64. Ibid., 80.

65. Ir. Const. Arts. 43, 45.

66. Ir. Const. Arts. 41–42.

67. Ir. Const art. 40, Section 6.

68. Ibid.

69. Ibid.

70. Section 2.

71. O'Callaghan, "Censorship of Indecency," 63.

72. Ibid.

73. Ibid., 60

74. Ibid., 61.

75. Ibid., 61–62.

76. Ibid., 62.

77. Ibid., 57.

78. Ibid.

79. Ibid., 69.

80. Ibid., 69–70.

81. Ibid., 71.

82. Ibid.

83. "Pay-TV Service in Trouble over Pornography" *Cable Europe* 2, no. 18 (Sept. 3, 1997)

84. Jennifer Stewart, "If This Is the Global Community, We Must Be on the Bad Side of Town: International Policing of Child Pornography on the Internet," 20 *Hous. J. Int'l L.* 205, 212 (Fall 1997).

85. "Pornography Banned on Net," *Irish Times* (June 14, 1997).

86. Uli Widmaier, "German Broadcast Regulation: A Model for a New First Amendment?" 21 B.C. *Int'l & Comp. L. Rev.* 75 (Winter 1998).

87. Art. 5 GG.

88. Widmaier, "German Broadcast Regulation," 87.

89. Ibid., 96.

90. Stewart, "Bad Side of Town," 241.

91. Paul W. Goldschmidt, *Pornography and Democratization: Legislating Obscenity in Post-Communist Russia* (Boulder, Colo.: Westview, 1999).

92. Ibid., 1.

93. Ibid., 66–67.

94. Ibid., 70.

95. Ibid., 66–67 (citing an October 1992 issue of *Komsomol'skaia Pravada*).

96. Ibid., 2.

97. Ibid., 135.

98. Ibid., 233–34.

99. Ibid.

100. Ibid., 170.

101. Ibid., 171.

102. Ibid., 139.

103. Ibid., 145.

104. Ibid., 149.

105. Article 242, Russian Criminal Code.

106. Goldschmidt, *Pornography and Democratization*, 169.

107. Ibid., 172.

108. Ibid.

109. Ibid., 173.

110. Ibid., 175.

111. Ibid., 176.

112. Ibid., 175–76.

113. See ibid., 145–46 for examples of some of the lawsuits brought against pornographers in Russia.

114. Ibid., 64.

115. Ibid., 224.

116. Ibid., 68–69.

117. Ibid., 212 (citing *Drasnaia Zvesda*).

118. Ibid.

119. Ibid.

120. Ibid., 69–70.

121. Wojciech Sadurski, "Freedom of the Press in Post-Communist Poland," 10 *East European Politics and Societies* (Sept. 1, 1996).

122. "Polish Parliament Approves Tougher Punishment for Pornography," Associated Press Newswire (Dec. 16, 1999).

123. "Parliament Outlaws Pornography," Polish Press Agency (Dec. 17, 1999).

124. Ibid.

125. Ibid., 233.

126. Ibid.

127. Ibid., 231.

128. "More Lenient Amendment Proposed for the Pornography Law," *Polish News Bulletin* (Jan. 6, 2000).

129. "Senate Approves Complete Ban on Pornography," *Polish News Bulletin* (Jan. 17, 2000).

130. "No Porn for the Polish, Says Senate," Associated Press (Jan. 16, 2000).

131. Ibid.

132. Ibid., 231.

Chapter Three

Asia

South Asia may have the worst record for violence against women anywhere in the world;[1] but Asia is probably the most sexually open region in the world, too. Many countries in Asia, with the exception of China and other communist countries, are known for their lax laws against pornography. Some countries, like Thailand, Japan, and, to a lesser extent, the Philippines and even Taiwan, have suffered epidemics of child pornography and teen prostitution. Indeed, Japan only recently made child pornography a crime. Many have legalized prostitution, sex clubs, and vast amounts of pornography both in sex shops, in movies, and on television.

While countries like Thailand, Japan, Taiwan, and Hong Kong are very open toward sexually explicit materials, others, such as China and South Korea, are much less tolerant. In China, for example, pornographers may face the death penalty, though some degree of pornography is tolerated and sexually explicit art and literature are legal. As for China, communism does not tolerate markets well, but even in a reforming China, a market in human flesh is unacceptable. On balance, however, Asian cultures tend to be less repressed toward sexuality. Still, even within each culture, there are groups who oppose pornography.

While it is one of the more liberal regions of the world, Asia is also an example of extreme contrast from nation to nation, some being strongly opposed to pornography while others remain amazingly open. Those that are predominantly Buddhist, rather than Confucian,

Catholic, or Muslim, are more liberal. Buddhism does not contain as many moral proscriptions toward sex.

CHINA

Legal Approaches

Producers of pornography in China are subject to sentences of thirteen years' imprisonment[2] or even death. In July 1989, the Communist Party launched a nationwide political movement named "Sweeping away the Yellow Subjects." "Yellow" means erotic and pornographic, as does "blue" in England and the United States. The campaign banned almost all written, audio, and visual publications that described any kind of sexual behavior. Publishers were arrested, and at least twenty persons were put to death for selling yellow subjects. The argument of the party and the government for launching such a movement was that the yellow subjects result in readers and viewers becoming sexual offenders.[3]

On December 28, 1991, the seventeenth session of the Standing Committee of the Seventh National People's Congress passed a resolution banning pornography by imposing even harsher penalties on pornography dealers. Aimed at safeguarding social order and promoting advanced socialist ethics and culture, the resolution against pornography stipulates the death penalty or life imprisonment for serious cases of smuggling, producing, selling, or distributing pornographic materials. The resolution stipulates that those who make pornographic materials available to people under eighteen years old will be strictly punished, indicating that some toleration for pornography exists even in China.

Public Opinion

While the attitude of the Chinese toward sexuality is conservative, books on anatomy or literary and art works containing sexually explicit material are not considered pornographic.[4] In Beijing from December 22, 1988, to January 8, 1989, and then in Shanghai between February 6 and 26, 1989, an exhibition of nude oil paintings was held by the Central Art College of China.[5] This exhibit was the first of its kind, attracting more than 220,000 visitors in Beijing and over 190,000 in Shanghai. The exhibits included 122 oil paintings. Only three were of the nude male. Most of the female nudes showed their pubic areas.

Researchers took this opportunity to survey Chinese attitudes toward the sexually explicit paintings. Applying a method of systematic sampling with a sample interval of every fifty persons, patrons were surveyed as soon as they left the exhibition hall. Thirty-six hundred questionnaires including twenty-four items were distributed to visitors in Shanghai. Of these, 44.7 percent (1,610) were returned.[6] Surprisingly, 59 percent of the persons surveyed had read or viewed illegal erotic literature. Only 1.9 percent of those who had read erotic literature, and 1.3 percent of those who had viewed erotic pictures, found the erotic materials distasteful. About half said they wanted to, or would like to, read or view the illegal materials again.[7]

In comparison, those who had not read or viewed erotic publications ideologically purified the paintings by minimizing their sexual aspects.[8] The author noted that this "purification," or seeing in the nude a political, pro-communist, or at least a nonsexual message, had become "a political addiction in China."[9] This probably means that somehow every artwork, particularly erotic art, is interpreted to support the communist ideology and the values of the government in power, thereby robbing the art of its erotic value and replacing it with some sort of utilitarian message about the art or about women's role in communist society. In this way, Chinese authorities repress Chinese sexuality just as they suppress political dissent.

Facing such extreme penalties, it is surprising that pornography exists in China at all. Racy novels, politically sensitive books, and "pulp fiction" are often produced by underground publishers and are standard fare at bookstalls in most Chinese towns and cities.[10] For example, since the 1980s, Guangdong Province has had one or two campaigns almost every year directed specifically against pornography, gambling, drugs, and prostitution. Police have even offered rewards for those reporting illegal production.[11] The campaigns, however, have consistently failed. The owners of hair salons, cafés, and dance clubs, the most likely places for pornography and prostitution in China,[12] all benefit from the campaigns, because the police actually clear the way for new pimps, madams, and pornographers, a change that actually keeps business flourishing.[13]

The reason for the reappearance of pornography after each campaign has to do with the kind of people caught. All the campaigns do is arrest unprotected prostitutes and their small-time pimps. The masterminds who really organize, coerce, and hold women in prostitution go unpunished or are punished only mildly, because they are protected from prosecution by public officials. Seventy to 80 percent of all Chinese officials may be corrupt, and those who are not do not have the political power to rule without those who are.[14] Once the campaign ends, the pornographers and pimps go right back in business. Even if the central committee and provincial authorities are serious about ridding Guangdong of pornography and prostitution, there may be no way to eliminate the enormous corruption without causing the regime itself to lose its own supporters.

As for prostitution, Beijing has tried a different approach. For example, China has 180 reform centers nationwide to house some forty thousand people a year involved in prostitution and pornographic activities.[15]

By the second half of 1994, pornography and prostitution still throve in Guangdong Province.[16]

TAIWAN

Taiwan is more tolerant toward sexuality than China. Until recently, prostitution was legal in Taiwan.[17] The city of Taipei hosts more than sixty sex shops, which sell a variety of products, including sexy underwear, condoms in different colors and styles, and erotic toys and publications.[18] Ninety-two percent of Taiwan's sixteen hundred pornographic websites contain pictures of children or adolescents.[19] As of 1993, there were no laws prohibiting minors from entering sex shops.[20]

Sex shops are not the only place Taiwanese children are exposed to pornography. Television programs in Taiwan are described as full of violence, crime, and pornography.[21] One study by the Television Cultural Research Committee examined a random selection of cable TV programs during a week in March 1998.[22] There were 267 episodes of pornographic programs found on three pay-per-view channels. Up to 45 percent of them showed footage of sexual violence. Of those, 25 percent consisted of rape-related subject matter, while 20 percent showed images of sexual abuse.[23]

A national survey was conducted by the Gallup Corporation in which 1,092 adults were interviewed between April 30 and May 2, 1998.[24] The survey showed that 87 percent of the respondents believe that TV programs are replete with violence, crime, and pornography, with 33 percent describing the situation as very serious. Some 60 percent of the respondents felt that violence or pornography is more prevalent on cable TV programs than on programs broadcast on open-air TV, while only 8.5 percent felt the opposite. Ninety-three percent of the people polled expressed concern that such programs will have an impact on teenagers, with 71 percent saying they believe the impact is major. About 80 percent of the respondents supported strong government intervention to reduce the amount of violence and pornography on the TV programs. Fifty percent of those surveyed answered that government intervention would not seriously inhibit artistic expression, while 32 percent said it would.

Efforts are being made to tame Taiwan's burgeoning sex industry.[25] The city of Taipei, for example, recently stopped issuing licenses to prostitutes, thus bringing an end to legal prostitution,[26] and the government recently launched an anti-pornography campaign.[27] Citing Taiwan's juvenile delinquency problem, the government confiscated more than 1.13 million publications and 192,932 videotapes of a pornographic nature.[28] Consequently, the number of advertisements promoting sexual services in local magazines and newspapers dropped from 106,453 in 1991, the year the government kicked off its anti-pornography campaign, to just 10,398 in 1996.[29] Finally, those convicted of operating child-pornography websites face up to five years in prison.[30]

HONG KONG

Hong Kong is also tolerant toward pornography, but perhaps not as tolerant as Taiwan. Pornography is often contained in mainstream newspapers and magazines.[31] The situation has caused worry among some parents.[32] A Boys and Girls Association survey of 325 parents found that more than 80 percent of parents fear their children are being exposed to pornographic literature. Only a minority of parents, however, have tried to prevent the exposure. The parents regularly purchase Chinese-language newspapers which most believe contain pornography. Half of those regard the situation as serious, yet only 30 percent of parents remove the offending pages.[33]

Public attitudes toward violent pornography are largely negative.[34] A survey by publishers showed that an overwhelming majority of people were against class 2 sexually explicit publications being featured at a 1998 book fair. Class 2 publications are classified as those containing violent, pornographic, and repulsive material.

Materials classified under the Control of Obscene and Indecent Articles Ordinance as indecent can be seen only by adults, but obscene materials are banned.[35] We were unable to find the definition of obscene, but one article suggested that pornographic comic books would have to be placed in opaque wrappers and not sold to children under eighteen.[36] Even video games are under attack. The Hong Kong Television and Entertainment Licensing Authority, under legislation that came into effect in December of 1993, has removed 20 percent of video games that feature graphic violence or nudity or in which seductive gestures are used.[37] Violation of the Control of Obscene and Indecent Articles Ordinance could land a pornographer in jail for up to three years and cost him a million-dollar fine.[38]

INDONESIA

Pornography has become a controversial issue in this largely Muslim country.[39] Adult videos and magazines are readily available.[40] Indeed, pornography appears to be one of the fastest-growing segments of the Indonesian print media industry.[41] Tabloids featuring soft-core pornographic material and hard-core pornography publications are widely on sale, albeit covertly. Some tabloids and magazines even feature topics like how to find child prostitutes and call girls. Although most of the magazines are tame by Western standards, protesters say they go beyond the limit of social decency.[42]

When authorities found a calendar called "Happy New Year 1984 Sexino," which was the first to show all-nude pictures of Indonesian women, protests prompted then president Suharto to order the Ministry of Information to take action against locally produced pornography in the media and films. The government renewed the war against pornography in 1994 when suggestive content once again became the staple of locally made films. More than forty titles were condemned as "pornographic" because they contained scenes showing simulated sexual acts; but millions of Indonesians lapped them up. Several of the films played to packed theaters for over two months. On the average, an erotic film screened in 1994 was seen by forty thousand Indonesians, four times the number of those viewing nonerotic films.[43] The availability of pornography has increased since Suharto's fall in May 1998.[44]

Surabaya is considered the center for the publication of pornographic media in Indonesia.[45] Because of strong protests from the community, erotica disappeared from the market for a short while. Publishers agreed to temporarily halt the publication of materials that could be construed as pornographic after police interrogated and arrested some of the chief editors responsible for the publication of erotic materials. Such reading material abounded in Surabaya prior to this agreement. As the criticisms have died down, pornography has reentered the market because the government has never imposed strict sanctions.[46]

Some label Indonesia's approach to pornography hypocritical.[47] Article 533 of the criminal code makes the showing or offering of sexually arousing objects punishable by two months' imprisonment. The criminal code has no definition of pornography but does have articles covering obscenity and indecency. The criminal code's article 282 on obscenity imposes a maximum of one year and six months' imprisonment or a fine of 4,500 rupiahs. One publisher was charged under article 282 for publishing photos using trick photography which made women wearing bikinis appear nude.[48] Despite the public's condemnation, there is no denying that foreign hard-core porn films and magazines are readily obtainable in most metropolitan areas in the country. This state of affairs has been tolerated for decades by the authorities. Meanwhile, kissing scenes are censored on television while gory sadistic scenes in action films remain untouched.

The Indonesian Film Censorship Institute is responsible for reviewing all television shows and commercials before they are aired. Censored are television programs with political content and themes related to ethnicity, religion, racial origins, and social groupings considered likely to cause social unrest.[49] Indonesian law also bans programs containing "violence, sadism, pornography, mysticism, gambling, and those depicting lifestyles encouraging permissiveness, consumerism, or that are hedonistic and feudalistic."[50] Also outlawed are programs that promote communism and Marxist-Leninism as well as those that incite conflicts or violate religious teachings, degrade human dignity or national culture, or disrupt the unity and cohesion of the nation.[51] In Indonesia, restrictions on political and religious speech may lead to restrictions on pornography.

INDIA

India has a growing problem with violence against women. Statistics prepared by India's National Crime Records Bureau show that cases of rape, kidnapping and abduction, dowry deaths, torture, molestation, and sexual harassment have shown a big jump.[52] One senior Indian official was quoted as saying that India and other south Asian countries had the worst record of violence against women anywhere in the world.[53] In 1997, India averaged 10 rapes per day.[54] In Delhi alone, rapes have gone up from 315 in 1993 to 544 in 1997. In 1998, until the end of September, 372 rapes had been committed.[55] The former president of the Indian National Commission of Women, Mohini Giri, says that a rape occurs in India every two seconds. Meanwhile, approximately twenty-four thousand female prostitutes are arrested and prosecuted annually.[56]

At the same time, India has little or no pornography. India's first pornographic television channel hit the screens in 1999 despite fierce opposition, but to little fanfare.[57] The Indian public remains intensely conservative. India's Central Board of Film Certification censors sex and violence from films. The censorship, however, has been described as "somewhat arbitrary."[58] Films are censored by the guidelines enunciated in the Cinemotograph Act of 1952, sections 293 and 294 of the Indian Penal Code, and the Indecent Representation of Women Act of 1986. As a result, police have even seized copies of *Cosmopolitan*.[59] These laws, one author says, weave a chastity belt around Indian cinema.[60] Yet, another author proclaimed that "on issues of liberty of speech and criticism of government or society, India has one of the most liberal censorship systems anywhere in the world."[61]

In India, the lack of pornography does not necessarily lead to less violence against women. Despite the *Kama Sutra* and India's idealization of women and sexuality, Indian women suffer severe sexual violence. The traditional culture, combined with India's oppressive caste system, may combine to contribute to the oppression of women in India. In this sense, the feminist critique of patriarchy may be relevant. Some feminists argue that patriarchy is the root of all oppression. It may be the strict, male-dominated, traditional culture that creates a social environment perilous to women in India. At the same time, freedom of expression regarding political and religious matters is fairly broad, indicating that India's strict restrictions on sex and violence have not led to the censorship of political or religious speech.

JAPAN

"The business of lust thrives all over the world, but Japan's mammoth sex industry enjoys a benefit pornographers and pimps elsewhere can only dream of: acceptance."[62] In video shops, adult tapes are displayed beside family movies. At least 12,600 strip clubs, sex shops, massage and shampoo parlors, and "love hotels," where rooms are rented by the hour, are reportedly licensed in Japan.[63] One study estimated that in 1994 Japan produced 14,000 adult videos a year, much more than the 2,500 new titles produced in the United States.[64]

Japan's up-front attitude toward sex goes way back. In Japan, sex and sexual relations are not viewed as moral issues, as they often are in Western countries.[65] Sex is viewed as natural, like eating, to be enjoyed in its proper place. For centuries the Japanese have celebrated fertility in festivals centering on phallic worship. Religious sexual taboos never took root. Prostitution wasn't even outlawed until 1956, and the ban has had a minimal effect on the business.

Approaches to Prostitution

State-sanctioned prostitution began in Japan around 1612 when Shoji Jinyemon petitioned Japan's feudalistic government for the right to build a red-light district in Edo, the capital, to be called Yoshiwara.[66] Five years later, the government granted its consent but mandated that the area be severely regulated. Regulations required the area to be walled, surrounded by a moat, and open only during the day. The size of the brothels was limited. They had to be devoid of decoration, and the patrons could not stay longer than twenty-four hours. In 1657, Edo burned down, but the government provided financial compensation enabling Yoshiwara to be rebuilt. This time, however, the government became more lenient, allowing the brothels to operate twenty-four hours a day.

To supply women for the brothels, brothel owners purchased girls from families in the countryside and enslaved them as indentured servants.[67] The practice continued until the end of the feudal era when, in the late 1860s, under pressure from the West, and without banning prostitution, Japan voided the indentured-servant contracts, thereby allowing women to leave the brothels. As a result, a system of room-rental schemes developed whereby the prostitute was considered an "independent contractor" and the brothel a "room rental service." By 1875, the national government reinstated indentured servitude. Between the years 1899 and 1901, religious groups and other social reformers attempted to persuade the government to abolish the red-light districts. Though their efforts proved unsuccessful, the government responded by passing the Regulation for Control of Prostitutes Act. Social reformers continued to advocate for the abolition of prostitution until World War II.

After World War II, many Japanese women became prostitutes to cater to the U.S. military. Tokyo alone contained 670 licensed brothels and 70,000 prostitutes.[68] Many local governments passed their own ordinances regulating prostitution, and some, most notably Tokyo, enacted ordinances outlawing prostitution.[69] Then on May 24, 1956, female members of Japan's legislature, having been given the right to vote and run for office under the new constitution drafted by the occupation forces, passed the Prostitution Prevention Act outlawing prostitution.[70]

Approaches to Pornography

Meanwhile, the occupying American military prohibited pornography. The prohibition on pornography continued into the late 1980s. Images of frontal nudity, pubic hair, and genitals were banned, and no sex act could be depicted graphically. Prosecutions, however, are now rare.[71] The number of obscenity arrests and convictions declined from 3,298 in 1972 to 702 in 1995.[72] Not only are images of pubic hair, exposed genitalia, and hard-core sex tolerated, but the government also tolerates bestiality, sadomasochism, necrophilia, and, until recently, incest involving real children.[73] The child welfare law prohibited child prostitution, but there were no laws against child pornography. Most obscenity cases now deal with violent rape, realistic and graphic depictions of torture, or other behaviors considered dangerous.[74]

This age-old tolerance—combined with undreamed-of wealth—has fueled a freewheeling multibillion-dollar sex business that caters to every preference and is available at a moment's notice. This reality, however, thrives side-by-side with a quirky puritan streak, the legacy of both the importation of Confucian values from China hundreds of years ago and the adaptation of Victorian morality during the Westernization drive of the late 1800s. The result is a contradictory mix of the outlandish and the uptight. Rape is standard comic-book fare, but photos of genitals are banned. Porn actresses chat about their work on talk shows, and there are even schools for aspiring strippers and porn actresses, but single women who live alone are assumed to be promiscuous. Nudity is common on TV, but kissing in public is shocking. Despite the general acceptance of sex, a sexual double standard exists. Women are generally expected to remain faithful to their husbands regardless of their husbands' behavior. In contrast, men are given far more sexual freedom.

The paradox is luridly illustrated in the adult-video business. To comply with Japan's vaguely worded obscenity laws, producers blur out pubic hair and genitals. An ethics commission composed of major studios screens and approves more than five thousand titles a year, but the fastest-growing sector of the industry is illegal— "independent" videos that bare all. Director Mitsurhiro Shimamura estimates that one thousand illegal tapes are produced in Japan each month, thirty-five new titles a day. "In principle, you cannot sell them without the ethics commission seal, but they do," said a production company executive who puts out five hundred approved porn videos a year earning him $31.7 million.[75] In Kabukicho, dozens of tiny video shops sell illegal tapes openly. They get around the law by stocking only approved videos. Customers choose illegal tapes listed in voluminous catalogues. The clerk phones a nearby depot for delivery. Police periodically crack down on pornographers who break the law too brazenly, but they mostly look the other way. "It's a crime, but the police don't really bother us," said one store manager.[76]

Legal Approaches

Japanese laws recognize six types of sex crimes. Public indecency involving the public exposure of genitals and incidents that "violate a sense of morality" (a charge often used against strip clubs that authorities consider to have crossed the line on the limits of lewdness); obscenity involving any practice or sexually erotic material whose preparation, sale, distribution, or display can evoke "uncontrollable or disquiet reason"; sexual assault; rape; constructive compulsory indecency (a charge used when a victim, due to his or her mental or physical condition, was unable to grant knowledgeable consent); and attempted sexual assault, rape, and statutory rape are all illegal.[77] Offenders are brought before a panel of three judges.

Laws are made nationally but interpreted regionally. As a result, judges are more lenient toward pornography in the cities than in the rural areas.[78]

Under the "juvenile protective ordinances," formulated in each prefecture except Nagano, items identified as "harmful for juveniles" are forbidden to be sold to minors.[79] There were some 20,000 items on this list in 1970, but the list has expanded to 37,000 in 1980, 41,000 in 1990, and 76,000 in 1996.[80] When an item is identified, authorities inform the publishing industry's Publishing Ethics Council, a self-regulating body. The council in turn advises its members to mark the materials for adults and advises stores to put the materials, usually a comic magazine, in an "adult corner" of the store.[81] The advice is often unheeded. The sex-comic industry often sells to minors and earned over 180 billion yen in 1990.

Public Attitudes

Even though sex shops in Japan are not permitted near schools or in cultural and residential districts and are prohibited from hiring or serving persons under eighteen years of age,[82] Japanese teenagers have an open attitude toward pornographic materials. A 1991 survey conducted by the Japanese Association for Sex Education found that 21.6 percent of male and 7.6 percent of female middle school students regularly read pornographic comic magazines; and a 1995 survey conducted by the Government Management and Coordination Agency found the number to be much higher. As many as 50 percent of male and 20 percent of female middle and high school students reported that they regularly read "porno-comics."[83] These students are not ashamed to admit using pornography.

A survey conducted in June of 1997 of 1,100 Japanese, 1,200 Chinese, and 1,000 South Korean students showed that Japanese students feel less guilty about watching or reading pornography than their Chinese and South Korean counterparts.[84] According to the survey by the Japan Youth Research Institute, only 22.3 percent of Japanese students aged from twelve to fifteen think they should never watch or read pornographic videos or magazines, compared with 93.1 percent of Chinese and 51.1 percent of South Koreans. Among older students aged up to eighteen, only 8.4 percent of Japanese youth said they should not watch or read pornography, compared with 87.8 percent of Chinese and 28.4 percent of South Koreans. "Japanese children's sense of guilt about pornography has weakened because there are abundant obscene videos and magazines around them," said Tamotsu Sengoku, director of the research institute.[85]

Child Pornography and Teenage Prostitution

Part of this abundance includes child pornography and teen prostitution. Ninety percent of the five hundred complaints received by a Tokyo city official in 1996 urged the city to outlaw sex with minors.[86] Prior to 1999, Tokyo and nearby Nagano had no laws specifically forbidding sex with children.[87] According to a recent report from UNESCO, the United Nations children's fund, there are over twelve hundred websites carrying child pornography in Japan, and Interpol estimates 80 percent of all such materials are produced in Japan.[88] "Japan has the worst record of child sexual exploitation," said Mayumi Moriyama, the chief sponsor of the child pornography legislation in the Diet, Japan's parliament. "Eighty percent of the child pornography distributed in the world is made in Japan."[89] The National Police Agency estimated that there were more than three thousand Japanese home pages containing pornographic material at the end of 1997, 40 percent of which contained images of high-school-aged children and younger.[90] Now, an increasing number of high school girls are turning to part-time prostitution.[91]

Many teenage girls voluntarily use "telephone clubs" to engage in prostitution.[92] In telephone clubs, men pay a fee and then wait in a room for a call from a woman, frequently a young girl. Once the woman calls, the two arrange a compensated date called an *enjo kosai*. Realizing their business hinges on a constant supply of women, telephone clubs allow women to participate at no cost. In addition, the clubs solicit women by advertising in magazines, in newspapers, on subway trains, and by direct mail. They also distribute flyers with the club's telephone number at train stations and hang announcement signs on utility poles. Thus far, these tactics have been successful in recruiting women and teenage girls to call the clubs to meet men.[93]

Japan, under international pressure, has only recently criminalized child sexual exploitation and pornography.[94] The law, which took effect in November 1999, makes it illegal to pay for sex with anyone under age eighteen, as well as to traffic minors for sex, and to produce, distribute, or sell child pornography.[95] The Diet backed away from making possession of pornography a crime. It left untouched the titillating magazines and adult comics read openly, many with explicit pictures of young-looking girls. Previously, police had to catch child pornographers shooting photographs or videos, which is prohibited under the child welfare law.[96] In addition to outlawing child pornography, the new law also bans sex with a minor under eighteen years of age both in Japan and in foreign countries[97] and makes it a crime to distribute child pornography or solicit minors for sexual purposes either in Japan or abroad.[98]

Whether the availability of graphic pornography has brought the social decay for which it is blamed elsewhere is unclear.[99] While women can walk nearly anywhere in Japan's large cities with little to worry about except for anonymous fondling by men on crowded subway trains, domestic violence is a major problem. Crime is low, with reported cases of rape, sexual assault, and indecency decreasing after Japan legalized pornography.[100] Other studies, however, suggest something entirely different. The rate of domestic violence may actually be rather high, affecting as many as a third of Japanese women.[101] Indeed, a third of the women murdered in Japan are victims of domestic violence.[102] Japanese women do not report the violence, because the Japanese Confucian culture "expects women to obey their fathers in childhood, their husbands in marriage, and their sons in old age."[103] Battered women's shelters are scarce and underfunded, and women fear retaliation.[104] Additionally, women's advancement in Japan lags behind that in most of the industrialized world. Women make up only 9.3 percent of Japanese corporate executives, compared to 44.3 percent in the United States, 30.6 percent in Norway, and 26.6 percent in Germany.[105]

PHILIPPINES

Pornography and sex in the media have become major issues in the Philippines. Pornography is becoming a large industry in this mostly Catholic country.[106] Under the Philippine penal code, those who "publicly espouse or proclaim doctrine openly contrary to public morals" may be imprisoned for up to twelve years or ordered to pay a fine of up to 12,000 pesos or 300 dollars.[107] Rapists face the death penalty.[108] Still, sex crimes are on the rise.[109] Thousands have taken to the streets to protest the proliferation of pornography in the movies and on television.[110] In response, then president Joseph Estrada launched a crackdown against pornography and obscenity saying he instructed the police, military, and local governments to confiscate all lewd and pornographic magazines and films and to file charges against the producers of these movies and the owners of the theaters that show them.[111] Meanwhile, the Catholic Church, lawmakers, and other civic groups have criticized the Movie and Television Review and Classification Board (MTRCB) for its liberal policy of approving films with total nudity and explicit sex acts.[112]

The Philippine Supreme Court, by limiting the power of the MTRCB, has been protective of freedom of expression. In the landmark case of *Gonzalez v. Kalaw Katigbak*, decided July 22, 1985, the supreme court held that the MTRCB could only classify movies but could not ban them.[113] The chief justice wrote:

> It is the opinion of this Court that to avoid an unconstitutional taint on its creation, the power of respondent board is limited to the classification of films. It can, to safeguard other constitutional objections, determine what motion pictures are for general patronage and what may require either parental guidance or be limited to adults only. That is to abide by the principle that freedom of expression is the rule and restrictions the exception. The power to exercise prior restraint is not to be presumed, rather the presumption is against its validity.[114]

The only time censorship is permitted, the court ruled, is when there is "the clearest proof of a clear and present danger of a substantive evil to public safety, public morals, public health or any other legitimate public interest."[115] The Philippine Supreme Court has followed the U.S. *Miller* standard in defining obscenity as material that "to the average person, applying contemporary community standards, finds the dominant theme of the material, taken as a whole, appeals to the prurient interest."[116] Still, the Philippines has high rates of prostitution, including child prostitution and pornography.[117]

THAILAND

Thailand attracts some five hundred thousand sex tourists a year. A study conducted at a Thai university estimated that 12 percent of the country's gross domestic product is involved with the sex sector.

According to one Thai screen writer, "Thailand has one of the freest presses in Asia, but Thai cinema is the most strictly censored in the world."[118] Thailand is the only country in Southeast Asia where censorship is handled by the police.[119] Written in 1930, Thailand's censorship law has not changed with the times.[120] Laws on defamation and article 287 of the penal code punish those publicizing obscene materials with three years' imprisonment or a fine of 6,000 baht. New legislation calls for an increase in prison terms from one to five years and a fine of 20,000 to 100,000 baht.[121] Thai authorities have even gone so far as to apprehend a webmaster who posted photos made to look like nude photos of famous Thai actresses.[122] All this seems amazing considering that Thailand is known for its sex trade.

Bangkok is famous for its strip clubs, prostitution, and child prostitution. Foreigners come to Thailand just to have sex with children.[123] According to the Centre for the Protection of Children's Rights, more than ten thousand foreign children are sold into prostitution in Thailand every year.[124] Many of these children are from neighboring Asian countries, but some come from as far away as Europe. While some argue that sex between adults and children is not necessarily abusive,[125] the problem in Thailand stems not from a lack of laws, as in Japan, but from a lack of enforcement encouraged by corruption.[126] Indeed, Thailand drafted a new constitution in 1997. The law provides for the improved selection of police officers, more education and training so as to prevent corruption, more support for good officers, including increased wages, more penalties for corruption, and more incentives for working in communities with more people involved in decision making, monitoring, and implementation through multidisciplinary teams to respond to children's needs.[127]

CONCLUSION

Asia's openness to sexuality is marred by the high levels of violence against women, women's subservience, and high levels of child pornography and prostitution. Some have described South Asia as "the most gender insensitive region in the world."[128] While some countries, such as India, have high levels of violence against women but little tolerance for pornography,[129]others, like Japan, have an abundance of pornography but little officially reported violence against women. Given the high level of child prostitution and pornography, the extreme fetishism of some Asian pornography, including bondage and torture, and the private nature of Asian cultures, there may be much more violence against women than is officially reported. Considering the amount of violent pornography in many of these countries, the actual amount of violence against women and children, particularly in the home, may be understated. Asian cultures may not allow for the reporting and prosecution of sexual abuse, as the victims may feel intense shame about the abuse. Reporting the abuse to the authorities may be discouraged in Asia's rigidly patriarchal cultures.

Perhaps Asia's approach to sexuality, while open, is unbalanced. This lack of balance may actually be common for cultures throughout the world, but each type of imbalance is different. For instance, Islamic countries may be considered imbalanced toward the repression of sexuality. In Indonesia, an Islamic nation in Asia, the imbalance is extreme. Erotica is historically a part of Indonesian film, but protesters decry it and lawmakers forbid it. While this may better reflect divisions within a nation, rarely do we find a culture whose approach to sexual intimacy is primarily loving and open.

Asia's approach to sexuality seems more neutral than positive. Asians, particularly the Japanese, simply accept sex as a natural act to be enjoyed. Their toleration for child pornography may indicate more than simply a toleration of those with different sexual preferences and fetishes. It may indicate an acceptance of male dominance in the home. Sexual use or abuse may not be officially legal, but unofficially it is tolerated. On the other hand, it may also be that ancient Western moral proscriptions regarding sexuality simply make us unable to accept what are otherwise natural sexual appetites, even involving children. Whatever the case, openness is not the be-all and end-all for healthy sexuality. Simply tolerating a wide range of behaviors may not be the ideal.

NOTES

1. "Women's Groups Call for End to Attacks on Thai Women: Anti-Violence Day Launches Crusade," *Bangkok Post* (Nov. 26, 1998).

2. "China: Illegal Publications Seized? Pornography Producers Sentenced," *China Daily* (July 16, 1999).

3. Sui-ming Pan, "China: Acceptability and Effect of Three Kinds of Sexual Publication," 22 *Archives of Sexual Behavior*, 59 (1993).

4. "NPC Enacts Laws on Drugs, Pornography," *Beijing Review* 7 (Jan. 14–20, 1991).

5. "Guangdong Offers Anti-Pornography Rewards," Xinhau English Newswire, (Dec. 13, 1996).

6. Ibid., 59–60.

7. Ibid., 65.

8. Ibid., 70.

9. Ibid.

10. "China Trumpets Success of Fighting Pornography," Associated Press (July 24, 1997).

11. "Guangdong Offers Anti-Pornography Rewards," Xinhau English Newswire (Dec. 13, 1996).

12. "China: State Hits Hard on Hookers," *China Daily* (Aug. 22, 1997).

13. Jun Dong, "The Protective 'Umbrellas' and Their Protectees," *Princeton China Initiative* 4, no. 10 (Oct. 1, 1996).

14. Ibid.

15. "PRC Prostitution, Pornography Reform Centers Set Up," *World News Connection* (Nov. 24, 1999).

16. Ibid.

17. Linda Chang, "Taipei Prostitutes Protest Termination of Legal Status," *Free China Journal* (Sept. 12, 1997).

18. Diana Lin, "Taipei Looks Closely at Sex Shop Quandary," *Free China Journal* (Nov. 12, 1993).

19. "Group Aims to Bring an End to Online Child Pornography," World Reporter-Asia Intelligence Wire (July 22, 1999).

20. Diana Lin, "Taipei Looks Closely at Sex Shop Quandary," *Free China Journal* (Nov. 12, 1993).

21. "TV Programs Said Full of Violence and Pornography," Central News Agency (May 13, 1998).

22. "Pay-per-View Stations Found Violating Obscenity Laws," *China News* (May 26, 1998).

23. Ibid.

24. "TV Programs Said Full of Violence and Pornography," Central News Agency (May 13, 1998).

25. "Pornographic Publications Destroyed in Public Ceremony," Central News Agency Taiwan, (Sept. 21, 1997) ("Tens of thousands of porno-

graphic publications, including books, videotapes and CD-ROMs were destroyed . . . to signify the government's determination to wipe out pornography on the island.")

26. Linda Chang, "Taipei Prostitutes Protest Termination of Legal Status," *Free China Journal*, Sept. 12, 1997 (stating only 15 of 129 licensed prostitutes expressed willingness to join vocational training program, and some sued the city under article 15 of constitution and article 304 of criminal code, which protect citizens' right to work).

27. Ken Chiu, "GIO Awards Pornography Fighters," *Free China Journal* (May 31, 1996).

28. Ibid.

29. Ibid.

30. "Group Aims to Bring an End to Online Child Pornography," World Reporter–Asia Intelligence Wire (July 22, 1999).

31. Connie Law, "Pornography Crackdown," *South China Morning Post* (Dec. 7, 1994).

32. Audrey Parwani, "Most Parents Fail to Act on Pornography," *South China Morning Post* (Aug. 1, 1998).

33. Ibid.

34. Geraldine Carrol, "Pornography Off the Shelf at Book Fair," *Hong Kong* (Jan. 22, 1998).

35. *South China Morning Post* (July 4, 1996).

36. Connie Law, "Pornography Crackdown," *South China Morning Post* (Dec. 7, 1994).

37. Jojo Moyes, "Fears over Video Game, Violence Link," *South China Morning Post* (Feb. 20, 1994).

38. "Judge Upholds Prison Terms for Porn Sellers," *Hong Kong Standard* (Oct. 9, 1999).

39. "Hundreds in Indonesia Protest Gambling, Pornography," Dow Jones International News (July 4, 1999).

40. *Jakarta Post* (Oct. 21, 1999).

41. Janet Steele, "Banning Porn Curtails Freedom of Expression," (Sept. 16, 1999).

42. "Hundreds in Indonesia Protest Gambling, Pornography," Dow Jones International News (July 4, 1999).

43. Ibid.

44. Gin Kurniawan, "Pornography Industry Surges in Surabaya," *Jakarta Post* (Sept. 10, 1999).

45. Ibid.

46. Ibid.

47. Ibid.

48. "Pornography Elicits Mixed Reactions," *Jakarta Post* (July 4, 1999).

49. Brillianto K. Jaya, "No Clear Resolution in Sight on Taming Sex and Violence on TV," *Jakarta Post* (Apr. 9, 1999).

50. "House Passes Sweeping Bill on Broadcasting" (Dec. 10, 1996).

51. Ibid.

52. "Women's Groups Call for End to Attacks on Thai Women: Anti-Violence Day Launches Crusade," *Bangkok Post* (Nov. 26, 1998).

53. Ibid.

54. Ibid.

55. Ibid.

56. Arvind Kala, "Petty Laws Create Major Problems," *World Reporter* (Aug. 2, 1999).

57. Ian Mackinnon, "Launching of Pilot Pornography Show on Television Goes Nearly Unnoticed," *South China Morning Post* (Jan. 22, 1999).

58. Ibid.

59. "Don't Want to Know," *The Statesman* (Mar. 9, 1997).

60. Nikhat Kazmi, "Does Indian Cinema Need a Chastity Belt?" *Times of India* (Aug. 8, 1999).

61. Aruna Vasudev, "Film Censorship: Is It Obsolete?" *Economic Times of India* (August 17, 1999).

62. Joseph Coleman, "Pornography Easy to Find in Japan—It's Even in Your Mailbox," Associated Press (May 31, 1997).

63. Milton Diamond and Ayako Uchiyama, "Pornography, Rape, and Sex Crimes in Japan," 22 *Int'l J.L. & Psychiatry* 1, 7 (1999).

64. Ibid., 9.

65. Andrew D. Morrison, "Teen Prostitution in Japan: Regulation of Telephone Clubs," 31 *Vand. J. Transnat'l L.* 457, 472 note (1998).

66. Ibid.

67. Ibid., 461–62.

68. Ibid., 464.

69. Ibid., 467.

70. Ibid., 469–71.

71. Diamond and Uchiyama, "Pornography," 3, 8.

72. Ibid., 8.

73. Ibid., 8.

74. Ibid.

75. Joseph Coleman, "Pornography Easy to Find in Japan—It's Even in Your Mailbox," Associated Press (May 31, 1997).

76. Ibid.

77. Diamond and Uchiyama, "Pornography," 4.

78. Ibid.

79. Ibid., 5.

80. Ibid.

81. Ibid.

82. Diana Lin, "Taipei Looks Closely at Sex Shop Quandary," *Free China Journal* (Nov. 12, 1993).

83. Diamond, 7.

84. "Japanese Youth Lack Sense of Guilt over Pornography: Survey," Agence France-Presse (Mary 14, 1998).

85. Ibid.

86. Coleman, "Pornography Easy to Find."

87. Ibid.

88. Martyn Williams, "Japan Begins Enforcing Law Banning Child Pornography," *Newsbytes* (Nov. 1, 1999).

89. Dong Struck, "Japan Tries to Squash Child-Sex Industry: Laws Would Criminalize Pornography, Prostitution," *Washington Post* (Feb. 11, 2000).

90. Ibid.

91. Morrison, "Teen Prostitution," 469.

92. Ibid.

93. Ibid.

94. "International Pressure Prompts Japan to Outlaw Child Pornography," *Yomiuri Shimbun/Daily Yomiuri* (March 20, 1999) ("Japan was also severely criticized at a 1996 international conference in Sweden as a 'distribution base of child pornography,' and was pressured to oppose the sexual exploitation of children for commercial purposes").

95. Struck, "Japan Tries."

96. Ibid.

97. Martyn Williams, "Japan Begins Enforcing Law Banning Child Pornography," *Newsbytes* (Nov. 1, 1999).

98. Struck, "Japan Tries."

99. Ibid.

100. Diamond and Uchiyama, "Pornography," 9–11.

101. Velisarios Kattoulas, "Conspiracy of Silence," *Far Eastern Economic Review* (Feb. 3, 2000).

102. Ibid.

103. Ibid. See also *Alternative Report to the Fourth Periodic Report of Japan on the International Covenant on Civil and Political Rights* (accessed Dec. 17, 1999) www.nichibenren.or.jp/hrsympo/jrt/chap7thm.

104. "Panel Seeks Poll on Violence against Women, New Laws," Japan Economic News Wire (May 27, 1999).

105. Ibid.

106. "Catholic Church Calls for Stepped-up Fight against Pornography," Deutsche Presse-Agenur (Nov. 8, 1999).

107. "Anti-Pornography Groups Threaten Criminal Charges v. Censors Board," Deutsche Presse-Agenur (Nov. 29, 1999).

108. "Catholic Church Calls for Stepped-up Fight against Pornography," Deutsche Presse-Agenur, (Nov. 8, 1999).

109. Ibid.

110. "Anti-Pornography Groups Threaten Criminal Charges v. Censors Board," Deutsche Presse-Agenur (Nov. 29, 1999).

111. Luz Gaguioro, "Estrada Cracks Down on Porno Movies," *Straits Times* (Oct. 27, 1999).

112. "Thousands Rally against Pornography in the Philippines," Deutsche Presse-Agenur (Nov. 8, 1999).

113. Ibid.

114. "Ban Pornographic Films!" *Manila Standard* (Nov. 17, 1999).

115. Ibid.

116. Ibid.

117. Jennifer Stewart, "If This Is the Global Community, We Must Be on the Bad Side of Town: International Policing of Child Pornography on the Internet," 20 *Hous. J. Int'l L.* 205, 212 (Fall 1997).

118. "Movie Industry, Police Crack Down on International Film Festival: All Entries Must Be Viewed by Censors," *Bangkok Post* (Sept. 19, 1998).

119. Ibid.

120. Ibid.

121. "Communities Can Help Destroy Porn Websites," *Nation* (Dec. 9, 1999).

122. "Net Porn Can Lead to Deviant Behavior," *Nation* (Jan. 21, 2000).

123. "Sexploitation: Child Sex Abuse Now a Global Issue: Transnational Crime That Ends in AIDS," *Bangkok Post* (June 2, 1998).

124. "Prostitution: Child Abuse Widespread: 10,000 Lured into Flesh Trade Annually," *Bangkok Post* (Aug. 28, 1997).

125. "Postbag: Why Condemn Paedophilia?" *Bangkok Post* (April 24, 1998).

126. "Address/Child Rights and Good Governance: Combating Abuse of the Child," *Bangkok Post* (June 2, 1998).

127. "Sexploitation: Child Sex Abuse Now a Global Issue: Transnational Crime That Ends in AIDS," *Bangkok Post* (June 2, 1998).

128. Ibid.

129. Ibid.

Chapter Four

Other Nations

CENTRAL AND SOUTH AMERICA

In the countries of Central and South America there is no real controversy over adult pornography, but as of 1999 child pornography is probably illegal in every country in the region, though many have lower ages of majority than the United States. Poverty leads to much prostitution, including child pornography and prostitution. With a 20-billion-dollar worldwide child sex industry, some significant portion of that industry is located in this region, but adult pornography is not a government priority.

Peru

Article 183 of the Peruvian penal code states that persons who sell or deliver objects, books, writings, or visual or auditory images to a person younger than fourteen years of age that, by their obscene character, can greatly shame the victim or prematurely excite or pervert their sexual instinct shall be punished with detention of up to two years.[1]

Chile

In September 1989, with a return to democratic rule in Chile, the National Television Council (CNTV) adopted rules and the mechanism for their enforcement (articles 12 and 13) to prevent "morbid violence, pornography and the portrayal of children or adolescents in immoral or obscene acts." Article 13 requires the CNTV to take measures to avoid the transmission of films that have not been classified by the Council of Cinematographic Classification (CCC) because they were not intended for general release. Films not intended for general release may not be shown between 6:00 A.M. and 10:00 P.M. Other films may be banned completely.

As of October 1993, 66 of the 118 penalties imposed on the television industry were for infractions involving excessive violence, the exploitation of suffering, pornography, or the depiction of children in immoral or obscene acts.[2]

THE MIDDLE EAST

Muslim nations that are ruled by Islamic law are generally less tolerant of pornography than most other countries in the world. For example, as late as 2000, pornography distributors and producers could face the death penalty in Iran.[3] Iranian censors are concerned with unveiled women, women whose robes do not obscure all body curves, and eye contact between the sexes. Egyptian censors are concerned with bathing suits, passionate kisses, sexy dancing, and sex scenes. Jordan bans sexual material. Indeed, Muslims generally discourage all pictorial representations as a form of idolatry. The acceptance of some degree of belly dancing in the more secular Muslim nations, combined with the requirement that women be veiled in the more conservative Muslim nations, makes for an interesting, if sometimes volatile, mix of approaches to sexual explicitness in film and art. Adding to the explosiveness is the fact that even where government fails or refuses to restrict materials, private actors have taken over. For example, extremist groups, such as Hamas, have taken to beating video-store attendants, burning down theaters that show "explicit" movies, and threatening actors and actresses with physical violence.

Islamic Legal Approaches

Almost all of the Arab states recognize Islamic jurisprudence as the principal source of their law. For example, article 23 of the Saudi

Arabian basic law proclaims: "The State shall protect the Islamic Creed and shall cater to the application of the Shariah. The State shall enjoin good and forbid evil and shall undertake the duties of the call to Islam."

Even when the government does not strictly enforce the Islamic legal concepts of blasphemy, obscenity, and public morality, under the Islamic legal doctrine of *hisba*, any individual Muslim has legal standing to sue an offender of Islam even if the plaintiff was not directly damaged by the offense. Aggressive Islamic fundamentalist lawyers in Egypt have used hisba successfully to sue actors, actresses, movie stars, producers, directors, writers, and poets for violating Islam by producing obscenity, pornography, or blasphemy. In addition, the Islamic legal concept of apostasy has been used to curtail artists' freedom in Egypt and elsewhere. An artist who blasphemes Islam by portraying prophets in a less-than-perfect light, by questioning or reinterpreting Islamic traditions, or by participating in the creation of "obscene" images may be accused of renouncing his or her faith. Under Islam, the punishment for apostasy is death.

"Iran and Saudi Arabia's constitutions state that 'all expression is free as long as it furthers the goals of the state and is not detrimental to the fundamental principles of Islam.'"[4] Iran's constitution states as one of its goals "the creation of a favorable environment for the growth of moral virtues based on faith and piety and the struggle against all forms of vice and corruption."[5] But the constitutions of Egypt, Syria, Jordan, and Iraq all promise the freedom to express oneself in any medium . . . within the limits of the law. This guarantee of freedom of expression is the opposite of that guaranteed by the First Amendment of the U.S. Constitution, which promises that freedom of expression will not be abridged by any congressional act. Arab constitutions create a freedom of expression explicitly limited by laws. Thus, while our First Amendment places freedom of expression above the laws of the nation, Arab states place their national laws above freedom of expression.[6]

Israel

Israel's laws on pornography have drawn from American, English, Canadian, and West German court decisions.[7] The Israeli test for

obscenity is the same as the American test: whether the work taken
as a whole has artistic value, or whether to the average person, applying contemporary community standards, the dominant theme of
the material taken as a whole appeals to the prurient interest. In
*Station Film Company Ltd. v. Films and Plays Censorship Board
and the Interior Minister*, the government attempted to prosecute
the filmmakers for certain scenes, two involving children. The Israeli Supreme Court ruled that any limitation on speech must present a "near certainty of damage to the public welfare." The court felt
it should err on the side of freedom of expression and wrote: "Once
the film is deemed art . . . sections of it cannot be isolated and
treated as pornography: Each section must be considered an integral
part of the permitted whole."[8]

In Israel, using a minor to advertise pornography is a crime punishable by up to five years' imprisonment. The similarity between
the laws in Israel and in the United States, however, do not mean
that the situation involving the availability of legal pornography in
Israel is the same as in the United States. In Israel, mainstream
newspapers contain pictures of topless women and ads for prostitutes. Mainstream newspapers in the United States rarely contain
explicit nudity, but some may contain advertisements for "escorts,"
many of whom are prostitutes.

AFRICA

There is not a lot of literature about pornography in Africa. In those
countries in which pornography is a topic of discussion much of the
concern centers around pornography's effect on young people, its
role in contributing to violence against women, the racist connota-
tions surrounding pornography and its availability, and the protection of African culture.

Kenya

In Kenya, for example, the Kenya National Association of Parents
has declared war on pornographic magazines containing pictures
of nude women.[9] The magazines cited by the association include

Life, Seen, Family Bliss, Love Dust, Emotion, Beauty N' Style, Passion, Spice, and *African Blues.* The association has lamented that these magazines have "polluted" the minds of the country's youth.

Nigeria

Nigeria has its own pornography industry. While some magazines simply lift pictures from foreign magazines, others have even branched out into film production. *Better Lover* magazine, for example, recently produced Nigeria's first officially acknowledged hard-core porn film, entitled *Better Lover Valentine Sex Party.* The National Film and Video Censors Board immediately announced a ban on this and two other films and told the police to seize all the pornographic materials produced and openly sold in the country. The director of the board, Demola James, said the board took the action to check the negative influence pornographic movies have on society. He also complained that the movies contained immoral and overt sex scenes that constitute a violation of sections of the decree established by the board. The films were being sold without prior submission to the board for registration, examination, evaluation, censorship, and classification.

Although Nigeria's constitution guarantees the freedom to receive information, section 37(2) of the decree states that the board shall not permit any film which in its opinion depicts any matter which is indecent, obscene, or likely to be injurious to public morality. The producers of pornography in Nigeria, on the other hand, argue that pornography is being smuggled into the country daily and no one is doing anything to stop it. There is a good deal of pornography on the shelves of sex shops throughout Nigeria.

Malawi

In the small country of Malawi, the nation's censorship board has ordered border posts to search travelers for pornography.[10] The move is designed to stem the perceived rise in rape cases and teenage delinquency.[11] There is a debate in Malawi about how far freedom of expression and speech should go as the authoritarian laws enacted during the recent dictatorship are dismantled. "Democracy does not mean ignoring the country's cultural values," the nation's president, Bakili Muluzi, said.[12]

South Africa

South Africa has also begun to address the issue of pornography. In a country where as recently as April 1994 photographs of female breasts could not be published without a censor's star covering the nipples, sexually explicit magazines such as *Hustler* and many *Penthouse*-style copycats are now sold in supermarkets throughout the country.[13] According to one writer, "In the old South Africa, prostitution and pornography were so heavily policed that even taking a peep at a girlie magazine could land you in jail."[14] Later in the same article, he wrote that South Africa's sex industry had been "burgeoning, pulsating and immensely wealthy" long before the new government's more tolerant policies were enacted.[15] While prostitution has not exactly been legalized, the government has become more tolerant of it, relabeling prostitutes as "sex workers," and the police now largely ignore the prostitution trade.

But the new openness may have its limits. In 1999, legislation was passed that would control the dissemination of pornography over the Internet.[16] The law is designed to protect young people. Child pornography has become a concern with the advent of the Internet in South Africa.[17] Other laws are being proposed to curb all pornography and "hate speech."[18] One group, Women's Media Watch, has accused the pornography industry of being racist and catering only to white Afrikaner males.[19] The group specifically complained about the treatment of black females in *Hustler* magazine to the minister of health. Muslim groups found a *Hustler* article, "Heroin for Allah," "offensive, insulting and derogatory."[20] In South Africa, there appears to be an emphasis on the racist nature of pornography as well as on its effects on youth.

NOTES

1. www.ageofconsent.com/peru.htm. (Accessed 1999).
2. www.brw.org/report98/chile/chilerpt—07.htm. (Accessed 1999).

3. "Iranians Approve Death Penalty for Makers of Video Pornography," *New York Times* (Dec. 21, 2000).

4. Toby R. Unger, "The Status of the Arts in an Emerging State of Palestine," 14 *Ariz. J. Int'l & Comp. L.* 193, 218–19 (Winter 1997).

5. Ibid.

6. Ibid., 193.

7. *Station Film Company Ltd., v. Films and Plays Censorship Board and the Interior Minister,* H.C. 4804/94.

8. Judy Siegel-Itzkovich, "A Plague of Media Porn," *Jerusalem Post* (Feb. 12, 1996).

9. "Kenya: Parents Vow to Crack Down on Pornographic Magazines," Panafrican News Agency (July 15, 1999).

10. Dan Langegeldt, "Malawi Clamps Down on Porn at Border Posts," African Eye News Service (June 14, 1999).

11. Ibid.

12. Ibid.

13. Ken Wells, "Nation in Flux," *Wall Street Journal Europe*, 1995 (June 9, 1995).

14. Tom Nevin, "South Africa's Booming Sex Industry," *African Business* (Dec. 1, 1998).

15. Ibid.

16. "New Legislation to Control Internet Pornography," Media Institute of Southern Africa (Aug. 24, 1999).

17. David Greybe, "New Act Bans Child Pornography Outright," *Business Day* (May 28, 1998).

18. "Political Pointers in South Africa: Outside and Above the Law," *Business Africa* (Sept. 16, 1996).

19. Stuart Hess, "Porn for Afrikaner Males Only," *Mail and Guardian* (Nov. 6, 1998).

20. "South African Porn Magazine Relents in Muslim Row," Agence France-Presse (Nov. 19, 1999).

Conclusion

Most nations of the world where sexually explicit materials are available have some sort of government-run rating system as well as laws regulating the distribution of pornography. The United States is unique in having an industry-run rating system, which many have argued is ineffective in preventing the distribution of violent and sexually explicit materials to minors. In regard to obscenity, some nations, such as the United States, allow juries to make the determination, and others, such as Russia, leave the determination to experts. Where classification boards are used, it is the board that criminalizes certain material by refusing to classify it, but the board's determinations must be consistent with the nation's courts rulings on obscenity. In contrast, in the United States, obscenity violations are identified by the police.

Contrary to the views of anti-censorship advocates, the United States is not more prudish than other nations. Instead, the United States is one of the largest producers and consumers of pornography in the world if not the largest. While other nations may be more tolerant of sexual explicitness on television, the United States is the "porn capital" of the world. In reality, the United States is more liberal in regard to sexually explicit materials than most of the world. Even considering Western nations, particularly Canada, Ireland, Germany, and England, all of which restrict sexually explicit materials to a significant degree, U.S. policies are liberal.

Even in authoritarian nations where restrictions are severe, pornography is available. In the countries of Eastern Europe recently freed from authoritarian rule, pornography is flourishing. A pent-up demand combined with an increase in organized crime has led to the proliferation of pornography, including extreme and illegal pornography.

Most nations are more concerned with violence than with sexual content, except for the United States, where most of the most violent films are produced and distributed. Outside of war zones, the United States has one of the highest levels of violent crime in the world. Likewise, the United States may be the media-violence capital of the world, too. Some studies indicate that in the United States, pornography and violent materials lead to crime and violence against women;[1] but in Europe, studies of crime rates in nations which have recently legalized pornography have not shown an increase in sex-related crimes. In Japan, the actual extent of violence against women may not be accurately revealed by crime rates;[2] but the statistics available indicate that the vast availability of pornography, including violent fetish pornography, has not led to a big increase in sex crimes,[3] while in India, a country that severely restricts sexually explicit material, violence against women is at epidemic proportions. These results appear, at first glance, to contradict the laboratory studies that often show a connection between pornography and aggression toward women.[4] These studies have identified violence, more than sexual content, as a factor in violence against women, but the combination of violence with sexual imagery had the strongest effect.[5] This may explain why countries that allow a great deal of pornography yet restrict violent media, whether pornographic or not, tend to see no connection between violence against women and the availability of sexually explicit materials. Indeed, some American R-rated movies contain more violence and aggression toward women than does pornography.[6]

Islamic nations contain little pornography. Many of the Muslim countries have laws explicitly banning all sex-related materials. Even where no laws exist, self-censorship is practiced in the face of severe threats and social consequences for violating Islamic morality.

There are certainly other cultural factors beyond the availability of violent pornography that contribute to violence against women. The most glaring example is in nations at war, where the normal inhibitions toward violence are lessened and the social repercussions against rape are all but removed. Other cultural factors may also be involved. While identifying the other causes of sexual violence is beyond the scope of this volume, one could speculate that a rigid social order, such as the caste system, may contribute to violence against women. While there are a multitude of causal factors in sexual violence, sexually violent media are likely a contributing factor.

On the other hand, there may be good effects of pornography as well. Without sexually explicit materials, it is unlikely that people would be able to openly and readily discuss sexual issues. Our openness to sexually explicit materials has also opened our minds to frank discussion as well as freedom for sexual minorities.

RECOMMENDATIONS

The evidence shows that nations throughout the world impose certain restrictions on sexually explicit materials. Many nations remain more concerned about violent materials than about sexual explicitness. The positive effects of sexually explicit materials do not extend to violent materials. Sexually explicit materials should, however, be confined to adult-only areas. It is important to respect the rights of those who wish not to be exposed to sexually explicit materials. Statements such as "turn the channel" or "look away" are simply too little too late. Likewise, nations also have a right to self-actualization or the freedom to choose their own way. This actualization may or may not include exposure to sexually explicit materials.

How much children should be protected should be reexamined. The assumption that children are disturbed by the materials is belied by the fact that at a certain age children actually seek out the materials. Whether or not the materials corrupt children may be more an effect of the culture's attitude toward discussing sexuality than the "knowledge" of sex itself. Children in Japan, for example, appear little affected by the material, although the actual effect the distribution of pornography has on the lives of Japanese women is undetermined. On the other hand, while most parents will be responsible when exposing children to sexually explicit materials, others may not. Most nations throughout the world restrict sexually explicit materials to adults.

Even though sexually explicit materials may not have the negative effects violent materials have, the United States allows even the youngest children to view the most extreme violence with adult supervision. The restriction in the United States should be revised. Sexually violent materials should be the most restricted, including slasher films which mix mildly sexually explicit scenes with extreme violence. Violent materials should be restricted to those eighteen years old or older. That restriction would be highly opposed by the movie industry, as such a restriction will reduce demand for those materials. Violent movies are largely marketed to teenagers. Sexually degrading materials should be restricted to adults only. Exactly how degrading materials should be defined is open to question, although one study defined it as materials that depict women as "anonymous, panting playthings . . . eager to accommodate any and every imaginable sexual urge of any man in the vicinity."[7] Finally, nondegrading sexually explicit materials should be readily available, and minors should be allowed to view them under adult supervision. Because the distinction between degrading and nondegrading material will be difficult to make, people should have the right not to be exposed to materials they find offensive or disturbing. These materials should *not* be broadcast publicly. But because such material may also have beneficial effects, it should be widely available.

It is entirely legitimate to have a public policy of encouraging healthy, loving expressions of sexuality over less noble depictions. Even if materials were not banned, governments should encourage, through awards, grants, and advertising, nondegrading, healthy sexual materials. The nation has every right to refuse to fund "art" which the public feels is harmful, disrespectful, lacking in taste, or incongruent with the important value of tolerance. The government could also engage in publicity that discourages violent and exploitative sexual behavior and encourages loving and caring interactions.

The development of a government classification board, as is used in most countries, has not led to the wholesale censorship of speech. An industry-controlled system cannot be expected to restrict materials so as to preclude access to profitable markets. But one possibility is to require debriefing immediately after the film and before the credits. This is an ethical procedure used by researchers after exposing subjects to such materials. There is no reason why ethics do not also require the film industry to debrief viewers after exposing them to violent or sexually degrading matter. Moviegoers may not find this sort of confrontational approach agreeable. They tend not to be aware of the effect violent materials may have on them. If it were understood that some people may be adversely affected, and that for the protection of everyone, the debriefing is designed to reach those who might be aversely effected, then moviegoers might be more tolerant of the debriefings.

The United States should establish a government classification system like that used throughout most of the world. More sensitivity toward women's rights will be helpful, but by protecting pornography, the United States is also protecting sexual minorities and promoting open discussion on issues of sexuality. A law-and-order approach is probably the last thing pornography addicts and pedophiles need. Treatment programs for those who desire help, are the best way to help those addicted to sex, sadism, or pedophilia, just as drug treatment programs are the best way to address the problem of drug abuse. Openness to sexual expression, combined with reasonable limits on violent and sadistic media, and a government policy that encourages healthy, loving displays of sexuality will lead to less sex crime without threatening freedom of speech.

NOTES

1. *Pornography and Rape: A Multistate Level Analysis* (1985).

2. Takamura Kaoru and Noda Masaaki, "Japanese Society and the Psychopath," 24 *Japan Echo* (Oct. 1997) www.japanecho.co.jp/docs/html/240404.html.

3. Milton Diamond and Ayako Uchiyama, "Pornography, Rape, and Sex Crimes in Japan," 22 *Intl J. L. And Psychiatry* 1 (Jan./Feb. 1999).

4. Michelle Chernikoff Anderson, "Note: Speaking Freely about Reducing Violence against Women: A Harm Reduction Strategy form the Law and Social Science of Pornography," 10 *U. Fla. J.L. & Pub. Pol'y* 173 (1998).

5. Ibid., 189.

6. Ernest Giglio, *Rights, Liberties, and Public Policy*, (Brookfield, Vt.: Avebury, 1995).

7. Dolf Zillmann and Jennings Bryant, "Pornography, Sexual Callousness, and the Trivialization of Rape," 32 *J. Comm.* 10, 16–17 (Autumn 1982).

Appendix

Comparative Regulation of Child Pornography on the Internet

Sherry Mitchell

The development of the Internet as a global commercial and information exchange medium has led to the rebirth of the child pornography industry, enabling pedophiles to access, produce, and distribute pornographic images of children worldwide. In March 2002 the FBI announced it had cracked yet another Internet child pornography ring in a sting called Operation Candyman.[1] So far eighty-nine people in the United States have been charged in connection with the investigation, and an additional fifty arrests are expected.[2] Among the individuals charged in the investigation have been two Catholic priests, two police officers, a therapist, and a school guidance counselor, and more than two dozen of those arrested have admitted to molesting thirty-six children.[3]

Operation Candyman began in January 2001 when the FBI launched an investigation into three Internet groups involved in posting, downloading, and sharing pornographic images of children.[4] All of the FBI's fifty-six field offices became involved in the investigation, and over seven thousand people who subscribed to the Candyman e-mail group, including twenty-four hundred outside the United States, have been investigated.[5] The FBI's new executive assistant director in charge of cyber-crime referred to the target of the operation as an "international ring of pedophiles."[6]

The global nature of the Internet makes it difficult for any one nation to effectively regulate it. Most European child pornography originates in England.[7] Germany is a major producer, the Netherlands and the United Kingdom are major distribution centers, and the United States has the largest consumer demand for child pornography.[8] Many governments worldwide have responded to the rise of child pornography available on the Internet by passing laws attempting to regulate Internet content, creating specialized regulatory agencies to censor content, and enforcing strict punishments against Internet users who access offensive materials.

CHILD PORNOGRAPHY PREVENTION ACT OF 1996

In 1996 Congress enacted the Child Pornography Prevention Act[9] (CPPA), which criminalizes images that "appear to be" or materials sold that "convey the impression" of child pornography, even where no child is ever used or harmed in its production.[10] The CPPA defines child pornography as:

> [A]ny visual depiction, including any photograph, film, video, picture or computer or computer-generated image or picture, whether made or produced by electronic, mechanical, or other means, of sexually explicit conduct, where
>
> (A) the production of such visual depiction involves the use of a minor engaging in sexually explicit conduct;
> (B) such visual depiction is, or appears to be, of a minor engaging in sexually explicit conduct;
> (C) such visual depiction has been created, adapted, or modified to appear that an identifiable minor is engaging in sexually explicit conduct; or
> (D) such visual depiction is advertised, promoted, presented, described, or distributed in such a manner that conveys the impression that the material is or contains a visual depiction of a minor engaging in sexually explicit conduct.[11]

Congress made thirteen detailed findings that justified banning both actual child pornography and computer-generated child pornography including: (1) that actual children involved in the production of pornographic material may suffer physical and psychological harm as a result of such abuse, (2) that pedophiles and sexual abusers often use child pornography to "stimulate and whet" their own sexual appetites, and (3) that the technological advances in computer and computer imaging render it almost impossible to distinguish between real children and computer-generated images of children involved in sexually explicit conduct.[12] Based upon these findings, Congress determined that protecting children from sexual exploitation provides a compelling government interest in proscribing both real and computer-generated pornography. Congress reasoned that pedophiles' sexual responses to pornography apparently depicting children might cause a pedophile to sexually abuse actual children.[13] Furthermore, Congress found that sexually explicit images of children might be used to entice children to engage in illicit sexual behavior, thus resulting in sexual abuse of actual children.[14]

CASE LAW

Free Speech v. Reno

In 1999, the Ninth Circuit struck down language in the CPPA criminalizing visual depictions that "appear to be" or "convey the impression" of child pornography.[15] The court found that these provisions violated the First Amendment because they prohibit computer-generated child pornography along with actual child pornography. In ruling that the CPPA was substantially overbroad since it captures material that has been accorded First Amendment protection, namely nonobscene sexual expression not involving actual children, the court found that the government had not provided any compelling interest for banning computer-generated child pornography.[16]

Since no factual studies establishing the link between computer-generated child pornography and the subsequent sexual abuse of children currently existed,[17] the court reasoned that "absent this nexus" Congress's interest in preventing the secondary effects of victimization of children could not justify criminal proscription of child pornography where no children were actually used or harmed.[18] The court was not persuaded by the government's argument that child pornography is used by pedophiles to "whet" their own appetites and to sexually abuse children, and found that to accept the government's position would be to criminalize the "foul figments of creative technology that do not involve any human victim in their creation or in their presentation."[19]

Case Law Split and *Ashcroft v. Free Speech Coalition*

In the United States the free speech provisions of the First Amendment do not protect obscenity, and therefore its production and distribution may be proscribed.[20] Although obscenity falls in the category of unprotected speech, the Supreme Court has held that possession of obscenity in the privacy of one's home is protected under the theory of the constitutional right of privacy.[21] Pornography, defined as sexually explicit material, is protected speech under the First Amendment and can be banned only if it is obscene.[22] Child pornography, which has been distinguished from other sexually explicit speech because of the government's interest in protecting children exploited by the production process, is not protected speech and can be proscribed whether or not the images are obscene.[23] Furthermore, unlike obscene materials, possession of child pornography even in the privacy of one's home is forbidden by law.[24]

The CPPA expands the federal prohibition on child pornography to include not only pornographic images made using actual children but also computer-generated images that do not involve the use of actual children, raising the issue of whether such images fall within the Supreme Court's definition of unprotected speech. The Ninth Circuit's decision in *Free Speech Coalition v. Reno* created a split in opinion with the First and Eleventh Circuits, which upheld the constitutionality of the provisions of the CPPA criminalizing computer-generated child pornography.[25] Both courts reasoned that the compelling governmental interest in "safeguarding the physical and psychological well being of a minor" justified the congressional ban on computer-generated child pornography because of the importance of "crippling . . . the clandestine child pornography trade."[26]

The Supreme Court settled the issue in its recent decision, *Ashcroft v. Free Speech Coalition*, agreeing with the Ninth Circuit and striking down as unconstitutional the provisions of the CPPA banning computer-generated child pornography.[27] First, the Court found that the CPPA was overbroad because it extends to images that are not obscene and therefore protected speech under the First Amendment.[28] Second, since no children are actually harmed in the production of the computer-generated images, the Court reasoned, Congress could not ban such images based upon the government's interest in protecting children from sexual abuse.[29] The Court rejected the government's argument that computer-generated child pornography is "intrinsically related" to the sexual abuse of children and found that the causal link between computer-generated child pornography and the subsequent sexual abuse of children was "contingent and indirect."[30] The Court also found the government's additional argument that computer-generated child pornography whets pedophiles' appetites and encourages them to engage in illegal conduct unpersuasive and deemed it an insufficient basis for banning such speech.[31]

The Court concluded that the CPPA was so broadly worded that it prohibits not only images that harm children but also legitimate literary, artistic, scientific, or political expression.[32] Citing movies such as *Traffic* and *American Beauty*, both of which contain images of minors engaged in sexual activity, the Court stated that the statute would chill legitimate artistic expression by proscribing "the visual depiction of an idea—that of teenagers engaging in sexual activity— that is a fact of modern society and has been a theme in art and literature throughout the ages."[33] This latest decision shows that the Court is willing to endorse expansive First Amendment freedoms even in the novel context of the Internet. In another decision made the same week, however, the Court upheld a federal law aimed at protecting children from pornography on the Internet.[34]

CHILD PORNOGRAPHY ON THE INTERNET

What Is Virtual Child Pornography?

Computer-generated or "virtual" child pornography involves morphed and computer-altered images.[35] Morphing technology allows scanned photographs not involving actual or identifiable children to be manipulated into sexually explicit images through animation techniques.[36] Creating computer-altered images requires scanning images of an actual or identifiable child and either cutting and pasting the child's head on the body of someone engaged in sexually explicit positions or using image-altering software to remove the child's clothing and arrange the child in sexual positions.[37]

Developments in computer technology have revolutionized the production and distribution of child pornography. There were nearly one million sexually explicit images of children posted on the Internet at the end of 1995.[38] Over eight hundred messages that included graphic images of adults or teenagers engaged in sexual activity with children between the ages of eight and ten were found in one week on just four electronic bulletin boards.[39] In response to technological developments, Congress enacted the provisions of the CPPA proscribing computer-generated child pornography along with actual child pornography. One of the important congressional justifications for including computer-generated child pornography is that these images are virtually indistinguishable from images of real children, and as a result the government would find it almost impossible to meet its burden of proving a real child was involved in the production absent the provisions in the CPPA.[40]

The Development of Child Pornography on the Internet

Child pornography was originally produced in print, in photography, or on film, which required commercial processing and distribution by mail, or through other clandestine networks such as magazines.[41] Shops that processed the materials could tip authorities when they came across sexually explicit images of children, making production of child pornography an extremely risky venture.[42] Furthermore, the methods of distribution made it difficult for pedophiles to obtain these images, and as a result the child pornography industry was virtually eliminated in the 1980s. The subsequent availability of camcorders and digital cameras enabled producers of child pornography and pedophiles to make amateur videos in their own homes with little risk of being discovered by authorities.[43] The Internet additionally provided ease in transferring information between pedophiles and anonymity, ultimately transforming the image of the child pornography ring from one involving only producers of child pornography to include consumers of child pornography.[44]

The Internet provides three principal advantages that significantly lower risks associated with the earlier production and distribution methods employed by child pornographers. First, the Internet allows for the rapid transfer of files and images.[45] Second, the Internet provides relatively high security to pedophiles through encryption technology and therefore limits law enforcement's ability to detect users who participate in online child pornography rings.[46] Third, pedophiles can maintain anonymity on the Internet through visiting chat rooms which do not require an ID to sign on, by rerouting through multiple nations to remain undetectable, or by using anonymous remailers.[47]

The Wonderland Club Investigation

In 1998, through the combined efforts of police forces in the United States, the United Kingdom, Germany, Italy, Finland, Belgium, Austria, France, Sweden, and Portugal, a large and sophisticated child pornography ring called the Wonderland Club was dismantled.[48] The club was a United States–based organization with more than two hundred members in over thirty-three countries.[49] The individuals involved included a law student, a medical student, a retired Air Force pilot, and a teacher.[50]

The investigation into this child pornography ring was a result of an earlier bust of a smaller child pornography ring called the Orchid Club.[51] Two members of the Orchid Club were arrested by authorities in the United States, and as a result of this investigation English police were alerted to the existence of another Orchid Club member in Sussex.[52] The police in England seized this member's computer, and computer forensics discovered evidence of the Wonderland Club on the computer hard drive.[53]

The Wonderland Club employed multiple layers of protection to deal with the risks of being discovered by law enforcement. First, the club required that a senior member sponsor every new candidate for membership.[54] Next, as a consideration for membership, the candidates were required to possess over ten thousand unique images of child pornography on their hard drive.[55] A formal membership committee would then review the credentials of the candidate seeking membership.[56] All of these steps had the effect of limiting membership to the most hard-core pedophiles.[57]

The Wonderland Club employed all of the advantages available through the use of the Internet to further limit the risks involved. Specifically, members knew each other only by their screen name, providing the members complete anonymity.[58] In addition, the club used a closed network to secure transmissions of files through the Internet, employed passwords, and used advanced encryption technology originally developed by the KGB.[59] Although multiple countries were involved in the investigation, authorities were unable to infiltrate the club's security and encryption programs and had to rely primarily upon wiretaps, records of online transmissions, and undercover participation in more public child-sex chat rooms to identify members of the club.[60]

Online Pornography and Pedophiles

According to the FBI's profile, the usual pedophile in the United States is young, white, and wealthy: a white male between the ages of twenty-five and forty-five, upper middle class, and educated.[61] Individuals surfing the Internet for child pornography have most often been military officers with high clearances, pediatricians, lawyers, school principals, and tech executives.[62] Although the Ninth Circuit emphasized the lack of any studies linking the viewing of virtual child pornography to sexual abuse of actual children, a study relied on by Congress in making its findings under the CPPA found that 67 percent of child molesters and 83 percent of rapists use hard-core sexual materials and that 53 percent of all child molesters admitted to using materials to prepare for molestation.[63]

Some critics argue that the Internet is creating a new population of producers and consumers bored with traditional adult pornography and may actually be building an appetite among pedophiles that could lead to more children being abused.[64] Through chat rooms, pedophiles swap pornographic images, share their sexual experiences with children, and participate in online sexual abuse of children.[65] This bonding between pedophiles results in "virtual validation" that is accelerated by the Internet because it quickly gives the pedophile a level of validation that ordinarily takes years to develop.[66] Conduct that would likely have been deterred by the threat of criminal penalties is now validated by other online pedophiles, leading to actions against actual children.[67] Additionally, the Internet makes it easier than in the past for pedophiles to contact children.[68]

REGULATING THE INTERNET

The United States

Regulation of the Internet in the United States generally follows a self-regulation model in which the government has a minimal role.[69] Self-regulation is grounded in the First Amendment principle of freedom of speech. America is an "open marketplace of ideas" and "individuals are free to sell their ideas and opinions, no matter how objectionable or offensive they may be to some."[70] Congress may proscribe certain activities to protect citizens from invasion of privacy, obscene materials or sexual exploitation, and other illegal or fraudulent activities, but suppression of speech must be done in the confines of the Constitution.[71] For example, most countries outlaw hate speech, but in the United States hate speech is generally afforded First Amendment protection.[72] This is because attempts to regulate the Internet in the United States are countered by First Amendment claims of freedom of speech. Countries such as France, Germany, and Canada, on the other hand, value individual privacy and self-esteem, and regulations to protect these values take precedence over free speech.[73]

The Communication Decency Act (CDA) and the CPPA are the two most important federal laws dealing with child pornography. In *Reno v. American Civil Liberties Union,* the Supreme Court considered provisions of the CDA that prohibited individuals from making available either obscene or indecent materials through the Internet.[74] Indecency is protected First Amendment speech, and the Court struck down the provisions of the act that prohibited the display of indecent materials as unconstitutional due to its vagueness and overbreadth.[75] The Court, however, has defined obscenity as unprotected speech and therefore upheld the provisions that prohibit individuals from making obscene materials available over the Internet.[76] Since the Court has also found that child pornography does not deserve First Amendment protection, making this material available over the Internet is also banned by the CDA.[77]

The CPPA outlaws the use of computer technology to depict what "appears to be" or "conveys the impression" of a child engaged in sexual conduct. Prior to the CPPA, the focus of child pornography laws was the conduct of the pedophile and the protection of the individual child actually abused in the manufacturing of the pornographic material.[78] The CPPA, on the other hand, is premised on the belief that children as a whole are harmed by the existence of child pornography and that child pornography, real as well as virtual, increases the activities of child molesters. In proscribing virtual child pornography, Congress shifted the focus of prior child pornography laws from the harm inflicted on actual children to a determination that child pornography was evil in and of itself, raising First Amendment concerns.[79] The Ninth Circuit in the *Free Speech* case rejected this reasoning.

The Protection of Children from Sexual Predators Act was enacted in 1998 to combat the solicitation of minors over the Internet and in foreign countries.[80] This federal law prohibits transmitting the e-mail address of a person fifteen years old or younger with the intent to entice, solicit, or engage in any sexual activity and further prohibits foreign travel by U.S. citizens with the intent to engage in sexual acts with someone under the age of eighteen.[81] Similar legislation has been enacted in countries that have a large number of citizens who are sex tourists; for instance, Australia made it illegal for a person to engage in sexual acts with a person under the age of sixteen while traveling outside the country.[82]

The United Kingdom

The United Kingdom shares the same interest with the United States in protecting children from pornographic material on the Internet and completely bans child pornography, including virtual child pornography.[83] A major difference in the United Kingdom is that laws there define obscenity based upon the individual who may obtain and view the material.[84] Obscenity laws in the United Kingdom provide that material will meet the standard for obscenity if the individual viewing it is likely to be depraved and corrupted by the material.[85] Since children are viewed as being especially at risk of being depraved and corrupted by pornographic materials, most print material would not be considered obscene because access to it is controlled.[86] However, because the Internet is not subject to the same controls as pornography produced in printed form, children can access the material more easily, and images posted on the Internet are more likely to be considered obscene.[87]

Under the child pornography laws in the United Kingdom, possession of an indecent photograph of a child is a criminal offense, as is posting child pornography on the Internet.[88] Indecent images that are stored on computer disk or in other electronic means capable of conversion into photographs and pseudophotographs are also illegal.[89] Pseudophotographs are defined as images, whether made by computer graphics or otherwise, that appear to be photographs.[90] This definition covers both an image that does not involve an actual child but is manipulated so that it appears to involve a child and an image that was entirely computer generated to represent a child.[91]

The United Kingdom, in addition to legislative attempts to suppress child pornography on the Internet, has also followed a self-regulation model. In 1999, the Internet Content Rating Association was incorporated in the United Kingdom by founding members AOL, IBM, Microsoft, Bertelsmann Foundation, British Telecom, EuroISPA, Bell Canada, and T-Online Germany.[92] The goal of the association is to develop and implement an internationally acceptable rating system for the Internet that gives individuals the ability to limit offensive or harmful materials.[93]

France and Germany

The French government views the Internet as an instrument for the propagation of American mass media that threatens French language, culture, and values.[94] Regulation of the Internet is aimed at protecting France's national identity, language, and culture through legislation, with little consideration of its global impact.[95] This policy was evident when a French superior court ordered Yahoo! to block American sites containing Nazi memorabilia so that Internet users in France could not access the material and to destroy all offending material stored directly or indirectly on its servers.[96] The court ruled that the websites constituted a "disturbance of public order" and that materials based on servers or sites in the United States violated French law by "offending the collective memory of the country."[97]

The Yahoo! legal battle is reflective of France's protectionist posture in developing Internet laws and policy. Prior to the expansion of the American Internet in France, a homegrown online service called Minitel already existed.[98] The government strictly regulated Minitel, outlawing pornography, racism, hate speech, religious sects, and gambling.[99] The French government, realizing that it was being left behind as the American-dominated Internet spread, embraced the Internet with the intention of imposing national norms like those that governed Minitel.[100] In 1996, a French citizen uploaded a banned book onto the Internet as a protest against the government's suppression of freedom of speech.[101] The citizen was arrested and charged, but it is believed that the arrest was actually spurred on by official dislike of the Anglocentric nature of the Internet.[102] In the current Internet regime, French law holds Internet service providers responsible if illegal material detectable by a search engine is discovered on their servers.[103] Servers and hosts are required to be diligent in locating illegal materials and ensuring that rights of third parties are not violated.[104]

Government authorities in Germany have also ordered Internet service providers to block access to offensive and illegal materials, mostly neo-Nazi or pornographic content on servers both inside and outside the country.[105] Under German law, Internet service providers that allow the exchange of illegal materials are held liable in conjunction with the source that posted the material.[106] Concerns about exposure to liability and prosecution under German obscenity laws forced CompuServe to ban access to approximately two-hundred discussion groups.[107] Although the ban was a voluntary move by CompuServe, the fear of prosecution under German laws affected four million subscribers worldwide in 147 countries with different standards of obscenity and freedom of speech.[108] In 1998 a CompuServe executive was convicted by a German court on complicity charges for illegal pornography posted on a website by an Internet user.[109]

Canada

Canada has a strong interest in protecting the welfare of its citizens, especially its cultural, ethnic, and other minorities.[110] As a result, the Canadian government has enacted stringent child pornography laws and criminalizes hate speech on the Internet.[111] Over 90 percent of Canada's child pornography is imported, and in 1996 police in Ontario seized over twenty thousand computer child pornography files believed to be linked to a child pornography ring in San Jose, California.[112] Under prior law only the distribution of child pornography was illegal, but now the production, printing, publishing, distribution, circulation, or possession of child pornography is illegal.[113]

Canada, in addition to the United States and the United Kingdom, bans computer-generated child pornography.[114] On March 14, 2001, the government introduced a bill that may be the broadest considered by any country in an attempt to crack down on the child pornography trade on the Internet.[115] In addition to Canadian law that makes downloading child pornography illegal, the proposed legislation would make it a crime to even surf the Internet for child pornography.[116]

Australia

The Australian government created the Australian Broadcasting Corporation, a governmental regulatory agency that monitors online content and has the authority to declare material on servers both inside and outside Australia "prohibited or potentially prohibited."[117] The agency is authorized to issue takedown orders to parties in all parts of the world, and by June 2000, thirty-one Internet sites had been shut down through enforcement of the Australian Broadcasting Services Act of 1999.[118] Although Australia has passed sweeping Internet regulations and officially monitors content on the Internet, for the purposes of pornography, Australian law defines a child as a person who is under sixteen years of age.[119] In the global environment of the Internet, this makes defining what constitutes child pornography extremely complex.[120] A sexually explicit image of a sixteen-year-old girl posted on the Internet in Australia, if accessed in a country like the United States, for instance, would be considered illegal child pornography.

China and Singapore

China and other Asian countries are suspicious of Western culture, and the open exchange of information provided by the Internet and embraced by the West is in direct conflict with the more subdued and guarded methods of communication found in Asian culture.[121] In addition, traditional Asian culture supports official enforcement of its values, morals, and economic order, whereas Western countries value personal liberty and individualism.[122]

The Internet is officially considered a business tool by the Chinese government and not a way to access pornography or communicate with friends.[123] Chinese officials exercise tight control over content, and the government requires all computer networks to register with it.[124] In addition, all international Internet access must be coordinated through the police.[125] A monitoring room was established to track, but not block, information from entering the country, and the Chinese online service provider and subsidiary of the Chinese news agency Xinhua allows only limited Internet access and screens all incoming information.[126]

Chinese officials have found it difficult to control access to the Internet. As government censors predicted, Internet users who have accessed pornography, and video clips such as "Sexual Fighter" have been found on university computers.[127] Concern for national sovereignty led the government to announce a moratorium on new users in 1996, and further regulations required Internet service providers and e-mail users to file with the police.[128] Failure to do so led to heavy fines and imprisonment.[129] As a result, a black market for old e-mail addresses has emerged so that Chinese dissidents and citizens can try to communicate without being detected.[130]

Singapore embraces Internet technology in business and children's education but has traditionally restricted news and influences from outside its borders.[131] The government controls access to objectionable content available on the Internet in the interest of preserving the nation's political, cultural, and moral values.[132] The government has publicly warned citizens that it will prosecute anyone who posts defamatory or obscene materials, and censorship of content through peer review and retaliatory spamming is common throughout the Internet.[133]

The Singapore Broadcasting Authority is the agency that officially polices the Internet, and all service and content providers must be registered and licensed by it.[134] The Singapore government has also enacted comprehensive legislation holding Internet users and online service providers legally responsible for keeping objectionable material off the Internet.[135] Because of Singapore's interest in electronic commerce, however, the government has relaxed controls on Internet access.[136]

Middle East

In a number of Arab countries that adhere to strict Islamic law, the government rigorously blocks content on the Internet.[137] The Internet is heavily controlled by state-owned telecom monopolies, ensuring that transmission of undesirable material to and from the country is prevented.[138] In these countries, the Internet is viewed as an "electronic conveyor belt for Western decadence and debauchery," which, if allowed to enter into their country, "would infect their religions, political systems, cultures and ways of life."[139] Generally, the Internet can only be accessed through censor-controlled servers that block out sites, usually pornographic ones or those deemed offensive to Islam.[140] However, technological innovations and the desire to bypass the censors make information control difficult, expensive, and ineffective.[141]

Saudi Arabia is the largest and most tightly controlled Arab state in terms of media.[142] At Saudi cybercafés, female patrons are asked to alert the staff to any site that fails to respect Islamic values.[143] In Iraq, government censors cut out explicit scenes of films shown in the few cinemas in Baghdad and also censor content on the Internet.[144] Citizens have accessed pornographic sites that slip past the censors, but these sites are blocked out when they are brought to the attention of staff at the Internet cafés.[145]

CONCLUSION

The Internet, despite attempts to regulate it, has become a haven for all kinds of controversial material, raising concerns about violence, hate speech, and pornographic or obscene content. Virtually all countries in the world criminalize child pornography and online pedophilia; however, attempts by individual countries to restrict objectionable materials available to their citizens have generally failed due to vastly different concepts of individual liberties, freedom of speech, and morality. Advances in computer technology will cause additional problems as nations disagree over whether virtual child pornography is illegal or protected speech. As tougher laws are enacted to combat the spread of child pornography, production, distribution, and markets shift. New demand is being met by producers in the Pacific Rim, Mexico, and South America, and despite the crackdown on child pornography in the last decade, bulletin boards carrying child pornography have been found in the United States, Canada, Mexico, Sweden, Finland, Italy, Thailand, the Netherlands, and Japan.[146]

NOTES

1. Cheryl W. Thompson, "FBI Cracks Child Porn Ring Based on Internet," *Washington Post*, March 19, 2002, A2.
2. Ibid.
3. Ibid.
4. Ibid.
5. Ibid.
6. Ibid.
7. Jennifer Stewart, "If This Is the Global Community, We Must Be on the Bad Side of Town: International Policing of Child Pornography on the Internet," 20 *Hous. J. Int'l L*. 205, 212 (Fall 1997).
8. George Ivezaj, "Child Pornography on the Internet: An Examination of the International Community's Proposed Solutions for a Global Problem," *Child Pornography Prevention Act* 8 Mich. *J. Int'l L*. 819, (Fall 1999).
9. 18 U.S.C. §§ 2251–2260 (1994 and Supp. 4 1998).
10. See §§ 2256 (8)(B) and (8)(D).
11. See §2256.
12. See Michael J. Eng, "Free Speech Coalition v. Reno: Has the Ninth Circuit Given Child Pornographers a New Tool to Exploit Children?" 35 *U.S.F. L. Rev*. 109, 134 n. 28 (Fall 2000).
13. Sarah Sternberg, "The Child Pornography Prevention Act of 1996 and the First Amendment: Virtual Antithesis," 69 Fordham L. Rev. 2783, 2798 (May 2001).
14. Ibid.
15. *Free Speech Coalition v. Reno*, 198 F.3d 1083, 1095 (9th Cir. 1999), cert. granted sub nom. *Ashcroft v. Free Speech Coalition*, 121 S. Ct. 876 (2001).

16. Ibid. (citing *New York v. Ferber*, 458 U.S. 747, 764–65 [1982]).

17. Ibid., 1093.

18. Ibid., 1094.

19. Ibid., 1091–93.

20. Dawn A. Edick, "Regulation of Pornography on the Internet in the United States and the United Kingdom: A Comparative Analysis," 21 *B.C. Int'l & Comp. L. Rev.* 437, 443 (Summer 1998) (citing *Roth v. United States*, 354 U.S. 476, 485 [1957]).

21. Ibid., 444, (citing *Stanley v. Georgia*, 394 U.S. 557, 568 (1969)).

22. See Ibid., 443–44. Obscenity is measured by the standard set forth by the Supreme Court in *Miller v. California*, 413 U.S. 15, 93 S.Ct. 2607, 37 L.Ed.2d 419 (1973), which requires the government to prove that the work in question, taken as a whole, appeals to the prurient interest, is patently offensive in light of community standards, and lacks serious literary, artistic, political, or scientific value.

23. See *New York v. Ferber*, 458 U.S. 747, 758 (1982).

24. See Edick, "Regulation of Pornography," 445 (citing *Ferber*, 758).

25. See *U.S. v. Acheson* 195 F.3d 645 (11th Cir. 1999); *U.S. v. Hilton*, 167 F.3d 61 (1st Cir.), cert. denied 528 U.S. 844 (1999). See also *U.S. v. Pearl*, 89 F.Supp.2d 1237, 1244 (D. Utah, Northern Division, March 6, 2000) (rejecting the Ninth Circuit's analysis and upholding the constitutionality of the CPPA's prohibition of computer-generated pornography).

26. See *Pearl* at 1243.

27. *Ashcroft v. Free Speech Coalition*, 122 S.Ct. 1389 (2002). Specifically the Court struck down the "appears to be" (§ 2256(8)(B)) and "conveys the impression" (2256(8)(D)) provisions of the CPPA.

28. Ibid. at 1399–1400.

29. Ibid. at 1400-02.

30. Ibid. at 1402.

31. Ibid. at 1403.

32. Charles Lane, "Law Aimed at 'Virtual' Child Porn Overturned: High Court Says Ban Too Broadly Worded," *Washington Post*, April 17, 2002 A1.

33. *Ashcroft v. Free Speech Coalition* at 1400. See also, Lane. "Law Overturned," A1.

34. Warren Richey, "Porn Cases Exacerbate Divide on High Court: Justices Are Split on Finding Right Balance between Free Speech, Community Concern," *Christian Science Monitor*, May 15, 2002. That case involved the Child Online Protection Act (COPA). The Court affirmed a test similar to the obscenity test in the *Miller* decision to

guide enforcement of laws regulating Internet pornography under the statute. See ibid.

35. See Eng, "*Free Speech*," 111–12.

36. Ibid.

37. Ibid.

38. Stewart, "Bad Side of Town," 207.

39. Ibid.

40. Eng, "*Free Speech*," 127.

41. Stewart, "Bad Side of Town," 210.

42. Ibid.

43. Ibid., 210–11.

44. William R. Graham, "Uncovering and Eliminating Child Pornography Rings on the Internet: Issues Regarding and Avenues Facilitating Law Enforcement's Access to 'Wonderland,'" 2000 *L. Rev. Mich. St. U. Det. C.L.* 457, 461 (Summer 2000).

45. Ibid., 465–66.

46. Ibid.

47. See Stewart, "Bad Side of Town," 215–16.

48. See Graham, "Uncovering Child Pornography Rings," 463.

49. Ibid., 462.

50. Ibid.

51. Ibid., 463–64. Orchid Club was a private, online child pornography group that shared sexually explicit images of girls, some as young as five. Thirteen U.S. citizens and three individuals from Australia, Finland, and Canada were indicted for participating in an online molestation of ten-year-old girls, even though only one member was present during the actual molestation. See also Stewart, "Bad Side of Town," 206–7.

52. See Graham, "Uncovering Child Pornography Rings," 464.

53. Ibid., 462.

54. Ibid.

55. Ibid.

56. Ibid.

57. Ibid.

58. Ibid., 466.

59. Ibid., 463–66.

60. Ibid., 464.

61. Madeline Mercedes Plasencia, "Internet Sexual Predators: Protecting Children in the Global Community," 4 *J. Gender Race & Just.* 15, 18 (Fall 2000).

62. Ibid.

63. Eng, *"Free Speech,"* 126.

64. Stewart, "Bad Side of Town," 217.

65. Plasencia, "Internet Sexual Predators," 17.

66. Ibid.

67. Ibid.

68. Ibid.

69. Lyombe Eko, "Many Spiders, One Worldwide Web: Towards a Typology of Internet Regulation," 6 *Comm. L. & Pol'y* 445, 451 (Summer 2001).

70. Ibid., 483.

71. Ibid., 464.

72. Ibid., 462.

73. See generally ibid., 465–74.

74. Graham, "Uncovering Child Pornography Rings," 467, and *Reno v. American Civil Liberties Union*, 521 U.S. 844, 870–80.

75. Ibid.

76. Ibid.

77. See ibid., 468.

78. See Edick, "Regulation of Pornography," 442.

79. Sternberg, "Virtual Antithesis," 2801.

80. See Plasencia, "Internet Sexual Predators," 27–28.

81. Ibid.

82. Ibid.

83. See Edick, "Regulation of Pornography," 453–55.

84. Ibid., 451.

85. Ibid.

86. Ibid.

87. Ibid., 452.

88. Ibid. See also Stewart, "Bad Side of Town," 220–21.

89. Ibid.

90. Ibid.

91. See Edick, "Bad Side of Town," 453.

92. See Frank Valverde, "The International Internet Rating System: Global Protection for Children, Business, and Industry," 20 *N.Y.L Sch. J. Int'l & Comp. L.* 559, 560 (2000).

93. Ibid.

94. Eko, "Many Spiders," 467–68.

95. Ibid., 468.

96. Ibid., 471–72.

97. Ibid.

98. Ibid., 469.

99. Ibid.

100. Ibid.

101. Amy Knoll, "Any Which Way But Loose: Nations Regulate the Internet," 4 *Tul. J. Int'l & Comp. L.* 275, 291 (Summer 1996).

102. Ibid.

103. See Eko, "Many Spiders," 473.

104. Ibid.

105. Ibid., 474.

106. Ivezaj, "Child Pornography on the Internet," 8.

107. Knoll, "Any Which Way," 287–88.

108. Ibid.

109. Ivezaj, "Child Pornography on the Internet," See also Valverde, "Rating Systems," 566.

110. Eko, "Many Spiders," 473–74.

111. Ibid.

112. Stewart, "Bad Side of Town," 219 and n. 92.

113. Ibid., 220.

114. See Stewart, "Bad Side of Town," 218.

115. News Around the World, *Seattle Times*, March 15, 2001, A13.

116. Ibid.

117. See Eko, "Many Spiders," 474.

118. Ibid.

119. See Ivezaj, "Child Pornography on the Internet."

120. Ibid.

121. Knoll, "Any Which Way," 292.

122. Ibid.

123. Ibid., 296–97.

124. Valverde, "Rating System," 559.

125. Ibid.

126. Knoll, "Any Which Way," 296–97.

127. Ibid., 296.

128. Ibid.

129. Ibid., 296–297.

130. Ibid., 297.

131. Ibid., 293.

132. Eko, "Many Spiders," 477.

133. Knoll, "Any Which Way," 294–95.

134. Ibid., 294.

135. Ibid.

136. Eko, "Many Spiders," 477.

137. Michael L. Siegel, "Hate Speech, Civil Rights, and the Internet: The Jurisdictional and Human Rights Nightmare," 9 *Alb. L.J. Sci. & Tech.* 375, 392 (1999).

138. See Stuart Wallace, "Cyberspace Waves Fail to Wash Away Gulf Taboos," 4/20/99 Agence France-Presse.

139. Eko, "Many Spiders," 475.

140. See Wallace, "Cyberspace Waves."

141. Eko, "Many Spiders," 483.

142. See Wallace, "Cybespace Waves."

143. Ibid.

144. News Around the World, *Seattle Times*, March 15, 2001, A13.

145. See ibid.

146. Edick, "Regulation of Pornography," 213, 215.

Index

ABA. *See* Australian Broadcasting Authority

"adult" magazines: display of, 25

adult videos, 2, 73, 75

'adult' web sites, 57

Africa, 92–94

African Blues magazine, 92–93

Afrikaners, 94

age of consent to sexual relations, 15–16

Agreement for the Suppression of the Circulation of Obscene Publications, 13

American Beauty, 107

American Civil Liberties Union, Reno v., 111

AO (Adults Only) rating, 19

AOL, 113

Arab states, 90–91

Ashcroft v. Free Speech Coalition, 105–106

Asia, 65–88, 81–82

Australia, 1–2, 16–27, 27; approaches to prostitution, 26–27; Broadcasting Services Act, 24; Classification Act, 23; Film Censorship Board, 19, 20; Internet regulation in, 115; legal approaches, 18–24; Obscene and Indecent Publications Act, 18; Official Film Classification Board, 20; Orchid Club investigation, 120n51; public opinion, 24–26; sex-video industry, 17; television classifications, 19

Australian Broadcasting Authority (ABA), 24

Australian Broadcasting Corporation, 115

Australian Broadcasting Services Act, 115

Australian Capital Territory, 20, 26–27

Australian Women's Forum, 22

Austria, 109–110

Bad Lieutenant, 42

banning books or periodicals, 45

banning child pornography, 104–5

BBFC. *See* British Board of Film Classification

Beauty N' Style magazine, 93

Belgium, 109–10

Bell Canada, 113

Bertelsmann Foundation, 113

Better Lover magazine, 93

Better Lover Valentine Sex Party, 93

"blue" subjects, 66

book banning, 45

Brave New World (Huxley), 45

Britain. *See* England; United Kingdom
British Board of Film Classification
    (BBFC), 37, 40
British public opinion, 42–43
British Telecom, 113
Broadcasting Act (England), 37
Broadcasting Services Act (Australia),
    24
Broadcasting Standard Commission, 43
Buddhism, 65–66
Butler, Regina v., 11, 13

cable TV, 68–69
California, Miller v., 3–4, 119n22
Canada, 1–2, 10–16, 16, 97; age of
    consent to sexual relations, 15–16;
    Charter of Rights, 10, 15; Child
    Pornography Law, 15; Criminal
    Code, 11–12; Fraser Commission,
    17; Internet regulation, 114–15, 118;
    legal approaches, 10–14; Orchid
    Club investigation, 120n51; public
    opinion, 14–16
Capital Territory (Australia), 20
Catholic Church, 8, 80
CCC. *See* Council of Cinematographic
    Classification
CDA. *See* Communication Decency Act
censorship, 101; book banning, 45;
    Central Board of Film Certification
    (India), 72; Film Censorship Board
    (Australia), 19, 20; findings that
    justify banning child pornography,
    104–5; Indonesian Film Censorship
    Institute, 72; in Middle East, 90;
    Movie and Television Review and
    Classification Board (MTRCB)
    (Philippines), 80; in Nigeria, 93; self-
    censorship, 98; Thai, 80–81; video
    prohibition orders in Ireland, 46–47;
    Video Recordings Act (VRA)
    (Ireland), 46
Censorship of Films Act (Ireland), 46
Censorship of Publications Act
    (Ireland), 45

Central America, 89–90
Central Art College of China, 66–68
Central Board of Film Certification
    (India), 72
Child Commission of the German
    Bundestag, 50
Child Online Protection Act (COPA)
    (U.S.), 119n34
child pornography: Canadian approach
    to, 15–16; case law, 105–7;
    definition of, 104; English
    approaches to, 36, 43; findings that
    justify banning, 104–5; German
    approaches to, 36, 50; on Internet,
    78, 107–10; Internet regulation, 50,
    103–23; in Japan, 77–78, 86n94; in
    South Africa, 94; U.S. legal
    approaches to, 4–5; virtual, 107–8; in
    western Europe, 35–36; Wonderland
    Club investigation, 109–10
Child Pornography Law (Canada), 15
Child Pornography Prevention Act
    (CPPA) (U.S.), 104–5, 105, 106, 107,
    111–12
child prostitution, 81
child sexual abuse, 15, 78
Child Welfare Law (Japan), 75, 78
Chile, 89–90
China, 65, 66–68; Internet regulation,
    115–17; legal approaches, 66; public
    opinion, 66–68
Chinese Communist Party, 66
Cinemas Act (UK), 37
Cinematograph Act (India), 72
civil rights approach, 1, 10
Class 2 publications, 70
Classification Act (Australia), 23
classification boards, 90, 97, 101
CNTV. *See* Television Council
comics, 76, 77
Coming of Age in Samoa (Mead), 45
Communication Decency Act (CDA)
    (U.S.), 111
Communist Party (China), 66
community standards, 1, 4, 12

CompuServe, 114
computer-generated or "virtual" child
    pornography, 107–8
Confucianism, 75, 79
Constitution (Ireland), 44–45
Constitutional Court (Germany), 47–48
Control of Obscene and Indecent
    Articles Ordinance (Hong Kong), 70
Convention for the Suppression of the
    Circulation of Traffic in Obscene
    Publications, 13
COPA. *See* Child Online Protection Act
corruption, 68, 81
Cosmopolitan magazine, 73
Council of Cinematographic
    Classification (CCC) (Chile), 90
CPPA. *See* Child Pornography
    Prevention Act
Criminal Code (Indonesia), 71
Criminal Code for the Russian
    Federation, 54
Criminal Justice Act (England), 43
Criminal Justice and Public Order Act
    (England), 43
cultural values, 94
cybercafes, 117

Delhi, India, 72
democracy, 94
Denmark, 35–36, 51
Dirty Weekend, 42
domestic violence, 79
Dworkin, Andrea, 4

Eastern Europe, 51, 58–59, 98
Edo, Japan, 74
Egypt, 90, 91
18 (Suitable) rating, 40
Emotion magazine, 92–93
England, 35, 36–43, 97; approaches to
    child pornography, 36, 43;
    Broadcasting Act, 37; child
    pornography in, 103; Cinemas Act,
    37; Criminal Justice Act, 43;
    Criminal Justice and Public Order

Act, 43; Indecent Displays (Control)
    Act, 40; Local Government
    (Miscellaneous Provisions) Act, 40;
    Obscene Publications Act, 37–38, 40;
    Obscenity Act, 37, 39; Orchid Club
    investigation, 109; Protection of
    Children Act, 43; public opinion,
    42–43; Video Recording Act, 40–41;
    Williams Commission, 17; Williams
    Committee, 42. *See also* United
    Kingdom
English liberalism, 53
erotic literature, 3, 54
escorts, 92
Estonia, 56
Estrada, Joseph, 79–80
EuroISPA, 113
Europe, 103–4; Eastern Europe, 51;
    Western Europe, 35–36, 50–51. *See
    also specific countries*
expert commissions, 54–55
expression. *See* speech or expression

Faces of Death, 41
Family Bliss magazine, 92–93
Fanny Hill, 3
A Farewell to Arms (Hemingway), 45
FBI. *See* Federal Bureau of
    Investigation
Federal Bureau of Investigation (FBI):
    Operation Candyman, 103–23
Ferber, New York v., 4–5
15 (Suitable) rating, 40
Film Censorship Board (Australia), 19,
    20
Film and Literature Board of Review
    (Australia), 21
films: Australian rating system, 20, 21;
    British ratings, 37, 40–42; censorship
    of, 93; Censorship of Films Act
    (Ireland), 46; Central Board of Film
    Certification (India), 72;
    classification boards for, 101;
    Council of Cinematographic
    Classification (CCC) (Chile), 90;

Indonesian Film Censorship Institute, 72; Movie and Television Review and Classification Board (MTRCB) (Philippines), 80; National Film and Video Censors Board (Nigeria), 93; R-rated, 98; U.S. rating system, 5–6

Films and Plays Censorship Board and the Interior Minister, Station Film Company Ltd. v., 92

Finland: Internet regulation, 118; Orchid Club investigation, 120n51; Wonderland Club investigation, 109–10

France: approaches to child pornography, 36; Internet regulation in, 113–14; Wonderland Club investigation, 109–10

Fraser Commission (Canada), 17

Free Speech Coalition, Ashcroft v., 105–6

Free Speech Coalition v. Reno, 105, 106

freedom of art, 49

freedom of broadcast, 48, 49–50

freedom of speech or expression, 37, 48, 91; restrictions on, 44–45

Freedom Union party (Poland), 58

G (General Audiences) rating, 5

German Internet Content Task Force, 50

Germany, 35, 47–50, 51, 97; approaches to child pornography, 36, 50; Basic Law, 48, 49–50; Child Commission of the German Bundestag, 50; child pornography in, 103–4; Constitutional Court, 47–48; Internet regulation in, 113–14; legal approaches, 47–50; *Mephisto* Opinion, 48–49; Wonderland Club investigation, 109–10

Giri, Mohini, 72

"Glasnost," 52

Gonzalez v. Kalaw Katigbak, 80

Gorbachev, Mikhail, 52, 53

The Grapes of Wrath (Steinbeck), 45

Grundgrens, Gustaf, 48–49

Hamas, 90

Happy New Year 1984 Sexino calendar, 71

hate speech, 47, 94, 113

Heffner, Richard, 6

"Heroin for Allah," 94

Hicklen test for obscenity, 17–18, 37

Holland, 36

Hong Kong, 65, 69–70

House on the Side of the Park, 41

Howard, John, 23

Hungary, 36, 51

Hustler magazine, 94

I Spit on Your Grave, 41

IBM, 113

Indecent Displays (Control) Act (UK), 40

Indecent Representation of Women Act (India), 72–73

"independent" videos, 75

India, 72–73, 81–82, 98; Central Board of Film Certification, 72; Cinematograph Act, 72; Indecent Representation of Women Act, 72–73; Penal Code, 72; rapes per day, 72

Indonesia, 70–72, 82

Indonesian Film Censorship Institute, 72

Inside Linda Lovelace, 39

"internal necessities" test, 12

Internet: 'adult' web sites, 57; child pornography on, 78, 107–10; pornography on, 68–69, 110; Wonderland Club, 109–10

Internet cafes, 117

Internet Content Rating Association, 113

Internet regulation, 17, 23–24, 94, 111–17; in Australia, 115; in Canada, 114–15; for child pornography, 50, 103–23; in China, 115–17; comparative, 103–23; in France, 113–14; in Germany, 113–14; in Middle East, 117; in Singapore, 115–17; in U.K., 112–13, 115; in

Western Europe, 36; X rating for Web sites, 24
Iran, 90, 91
Iraq, 91, 117
Ireland, 35, 44–47, 97; Censorship of Films Act, 46; Censorship of Publications Act, 45; legal approaches, 44–47; video prohibition orders, 46–47; Video Recordings Act (VRA), 46
Islamic countries, 82, 90–92, 98; Internet regulation, 117; legal approaches, 90–91
Israel, 1, 91–92
Italy: Internet regulation, 118; obscenity laws, 36; Wonderland Club investigation, 109–10

James, Demola, 93
Japan, 65, 73–78, 79, 81–82, 82, 99–100; approaches to pornography, 75–76; approaches to prostitution, 74; child pornography in, 77–78, 86n94; Child Welfare Law, 75, 78; Internet regulation, 118; Juvenile Protective Ordinances, 76; legal approaches, 76; Prostitution Prevention Law, 74; public attitudes, 77; Publishing Ethics Council, 76; Regulation for Control of Prostitutes Act, 74; sex business in, 75; teenage prostitution in, 77–78; violence against women in, 98
Jinyemon, Shoji, 74
Johnson Commission (U.S.), 17
Jordan, 90, 91
Juvenile Protective Ordinances (Japan), 76

Kalaw Katigbak, Gonzalez v., 80
Keegstra, Regina v., 30n82
Kenya, 92–93
Kenya National Association of Parents, 92–93
Kwasniewski, Aleksander, 58

Lady Chatterley's Lover, 3
legal approaches: Australian, 18–24; Canadian, 10–14; case law, 105–7; Chinese, 66; English, 36–39; German, 47–50; Irish, 44–47; Islamic, 90–91; Italian, 36; Japanese, 76; Russian, 52–55; U.S., 2–5
legalization of pornography, 79, 98
liberalism, English, 53
Life magazine, 92–93
literary works: banning, 45
Local Government (Miscellaneous Provisions) Act (UK), 40
Love Dust magazine, 92–93

M (Mature) rating, 19
MacKinnon, Catherine, 4
Malawi, 93–94
Mann, Klaus: *Mephisto,* 48–49
Mayfair magazine, 21
media violence, 98
Meese Commission (U.S.), 17
Mephisto (Mann), 48–49
Mexico, 118
Microsoft, 113
Middle East, 90–92; Internet regulation in, 117. *See also specific countries*
Miller v. California, 3–4, 119n22; test for obscenity, 80, 119n22
Minitel, 114
Missouri, 5
Monitoring Report (Broadcasting Standard Commission), 43
Moriyama, Mayumi, 78
Motion Picture Association of America (MPAA), 5
Movie and Television Review and Classification Board (MTRCB) (Philippines), 80
movies: Australian rating system, 20, 21; British ratings, 37, 40–42; censorship of, 93; Censorship of Films Act (Ireland), 46; Central Board of Film Certification (India), 72; classification boards for, 101;

Council of Cinematographic Classification (CCC) (Chile), 90; Indonesian Film Censorship Institute, 72; National Film and Video Censors Board (Nigeria), 93; R-rated, 98; *Station Film Company Ltd. v. Films and Plays Censorship Board and the Interior Minister,* 92; U.S. rating system, 5–6
MPAA. *See* Motion Picture Association of America
MTRCB. *See* Movie and Television Review and Classification Board
Muluzi, Bakili, 94
Muslim nations, 90–92, 98

National Film and Video Censors Board (Nigeria), 93
National People's Congress (NPC) (China), 66
Nazi hate speech, 47, 113
NC-17 (No Children under 17) rating, 5, 6
Netherlands, 35–36, 51; child pornography in, 103–4; Internet regulation, 118
New South Wales (Australia), 26–27
New York v. Ferber, 4–5
Nigeria, 93
Northern Territory (Australia), 20, 22, 26–27

Oakes, R v., 10–11
Obscene and Indecent Publications Act (Australia), 18
Obscene Publications Act (UK), 37–38, 40
obscenity: "appeal-to-the-prurient-interest" requirement for, 3; concept of, 1; definition of, 37, 97; *Hicklen* test for, 3, 17–18, 37; "internal necessities" test for, 12; Israeli test for, 91–92; *Miller* test for, 3–4, 80, 119n22; *Roth* requirement for, 3; "undue exploitation" test, 12

Obscenity Act (UK), 37, 39
Official Film Classification Board (Australia), 20
online child pornography, 78, 107–10
online pornography, 57, 68–69, 110
openness, 82
Operation Candyman, 103–23
Orchid Club, 109, 120n51

Pacific Rim, 118
Passion magazine, 92–93
pedophiles, 110
Penthouse magazine, 21
Peru, 89
PG (Parental Guidance) rating, 19, 40
PG (Parental Guidance Suggested) rating, 5
PG-13 (Parents Strongly Cautioned) rating, 5
Philippines, 1, 65, 79–80
Playboy magazine, 2, 21, 25, 44, 57
Poland, 57–58
Polish Peasant Party, 58
porno-comics, 77
pornography, 51; definition of, 4; as hate propaganda, 4; legal definition of, 54–55; legalization of, 79, 98; online, 110; television channels, 72. *See also* child pornography; obscenity
Portugal, 109–10
Potter, Hugh, 24
propaganda, Nazi, 47
prostitution: approaches to, 26–27; child, 81; in China, 68; Japanese approaches to, 74; Regulation for Control of Prostitutes Act (Japan), 74; state-sanctioned, 74; teenage, 77–78; Telephone Clubs, 78; underage, 51–52
Prostitution Prevention Law (Japan), 74
Protection of Children Act (England), 43
Protection of Children from Sexual Predators Act (U.S.), 112

Protestants, 8–9
"public good" defense, 39
public opinion: Australian, 24–26;
    British, 42–43; Canadian, 14–16;
    Chinese, 66–68; Japanese attitudes,
    77; Russian, 55–57; U.S., 6–10
Publishing Ethics Council (Japan), 76
"pulp fiction," 67
purification, 67

Queensland Territory (Australia), 22,
    26–27

R. v. Hicklin, 37
R (Restricted) rating, 5, 6, 21–22, 23, 98
R v. Oakes, 10–11
R18 (Restricted) rating, 40
ratings, 97; 12 (Suitable), 40; 15
    (Suitable), 40; 18 (Suitable), 40; AO
    (Adults Only), 19; Australian system,
    19, 20, 21; British system, 37,
    40–42; Council of Cinematographic
    Classification (CCC) (Chile), 90; G
    (General Audiences), 5; Internet
    Content Rating Association, 113; M
    (Mature), 19; Movie and Television
    Review and Classification Board
    (MTRCB) (Philippines), 80; NC-17
    (No Children under 17), 5, 6; PG
    (Parental Guidance), 19, 40; PG
    (Parental Guidance Suggested), 5;
    PG-13 (Parents Strongly Cautioned),
    5; R (Restricted), 5, 6, 21–22, 23, 98;
    R18 (Restricted), 40; U (Universal),
    40; U.S. system, 5–6; X, 5, 6, 19–20,
    22, 23, 24
recommendations, 99–101
Red Hot Video, Regina v., 13
red light districts, 74
Regina v. Butler, 11, 13
Regina v. Keegstra, 30n82
Regina v. Red Hot Video, 13
regulation, Internet, 111–117
Regulation for Control of Prostitutes
    Act (Japan), 74

Reno, Free Speech Coalition v., 105,
    106
Reno v. American Civil Liberties Union,
    111
Reservoir Dogs, 42
Roth v. United States, 2–3
Russia, 51–57, 97; legal approaches,
    52–55; public opinion, 55–57

Saudi Arabia, 91; Basic Law, 90–91;
    Internet regulation in, 117
Seen magazine, 92–93
self-censorship, 98
self-regulation, 23–24
Sengoku, Tamotsu, 77
Sex and Sensibility (Broadcasting
    Standard Commission), 43
sex business, 75
sex comic industry, 76, 77
sex shops, 68–69
sex tourism, 80
sex-video industry, 17
sex workers, 94
sexual abuse, child, 15, 78
Sexual Fighter, 116
sexual relations: age of consent to,
    15–16; behaviors allowed in X
    category, 19; exploitation of, 11, 12;
    U.S. public opinion on, 8
sexual violence, 8, 73
sexuality, healthy, 82, 99–100
Shariah, 91
Shimamura, Mitsurhiro, 75
The Silence of the Lambs, 42
Singapore, 115–117
Singapore Broadcasting Authority, 116
Solidarity Election Action party
    (Poland), 58
South Africa, 94
South America, 89–90, 118
South Asia, 65, 81–82
South Australia, 26–27
South Korea, 65
speech or expression: *Ashcroft v. Free
    Speech Coalition*, 105–6; *Free*

Speech Coalition v. Reno, 105, 106; freedom of, 37, 48, 91; hate speech, 94; Nazi hate speech, 47, 113; restrictions on, 91
Spice magazine, 92–93
SPID-Info, 56–57
Station Film Company Ltd. v. Films and Plays Censorship Board and the Interior Minister, 92
Stephen Hero (Joyce), 45
Surabaya, Indonesia, 71
Sweden, 35–36, 51; Internet regulation, 118; Wonderland Club investigation, 109–10
Syria, 91

T-Online Germany, 113
Taiwan, 65, 68–69
Tasmania, 26–27
teenage prostitution, 77–78
Telephone Clubs, 78
television, 68–69; Australian classifications, 19; Indonesian Film Censorship Institute, 72; Movie and Television Review and Classification Board (MTRCB) (Philippines), 80; pornography channels, 72; public opinion on, 42–43
Television and Entertainment Licensing Authority (TELA) (Hong Kong), 70
Television Council (CNTV) (Chile), 89–90
Thailand, 65, 80–81, 118
Time Square Cinema Ltd., 12
Tokyo, Japan, 74
tolerance, 82
Traffic, 107
Tropic of Cancer, 3
12 (Suitable) rating, 40

U (Universal) rating, 40
"undue exploitation" test, 12

United Kingdom: child pornography, 104; Internet regulation, 112–13, 115; Wonderland Club investigation, 109–110. *See also* England
United States, 1–2, 2–9, 16, 51, 97, 98; Child Online Protection Act (COPA), 119n34; Child Pornography Prevention Act (CPPA), 104–5, 111–12; Communication Decency Act (CDA), 111; Constitution, 2, 4; Internet regulation, 111–12, 118; Johnson Commission, 17; legal approaches, 2–5; Meese Commission, 17; movie rating system, 5–6; Operation Candyman, 103; Orchid Club investigation, 109, 120n51; Protection of Children from Sexual Predators Act, 112; public opinion, 6–10; recommendations for, 101; *Roth v. United States,* 2–3; Wonderland Club investigation, 109–10

values, cultural, 94
Victoria (Australia), 26–27
video games, 70
Video Recording Act (UK), 40–41
Video Recordings Act (VRA) (Ireland), 46
videos: adult, 2, 73, 75; Australian classification scheme, 19; Australian sex-video industry, 17; classification of, 41–42; "independent," 75; National Film and Video Censors Board (Nigeria), 93; video prohibition orders in Ireland, 46–47; violence against video store owners, 90; X-rated, 17, 19–20, 23, 25
viewpoint discrimination, 4
violence: cult of, 53; domestic, 79; media, 98; sexual, 8, 73; against video store owners, 90; against women, 65, 72, 73, 79, 98
virtual child pornography, 107–8

Wales, 37
Watt (Beckett), 45
Web sites, 24, 78. *See also* Internet
    regulation
West Germany, 35
Western Australia, 26–27
Western Europe, 35–36, 50–51
Williams Commission (Britain), 17
Williams Committee (Britain), 42
women: corporate executives, 79;
    Indecent Representation of Women
    Act (India), 72–73; U.S., 9;
    violence against, 65, 72, 73, 79, 98

Women's Media Watch, 94
Wonderland Club investigation, 109–10

X-rated videos, 17, 25
X rating: Australian, 19–20, 22, 23;
    U.S., 5, 6; for Web sites, 24
Xinhua, 116

Yahoo!, 113, 114
"yellow" subjects, 66
Yeltsin, Boris, 52, 54
Yoshiwara (Edo, Japan), 74

About the Authors

RICHARD PROCIDA is currently a graduate student at American University's School of International Service. He received a Bachelor of Science from the University of Southern California where he majored in international relations and social sciences with a minor in The Study of Women and Men in Society, USC's gender studies program.

He was active in the feminist movement prior to attending law school. He gave presentations on pornography before groups and at colleges throughout southern California. He also wrote two opinion articles related to pornography for the *Los Angeles Daily Journal*, and authored a chapter entiled "A Pattern for Change" published on the Internet in a book for men recovering from pornography addiction.

No longer active in the feminist movement, Procida is an attorney who runs his own law practice in Whittier, California. He handles civil rights and employment cases as well as administrative and consumer law claims.

RITA J. SIMON is a sociologist who earned her doctorate at the University of Chicago in 1957. Before coming to American University in 1983 to serve as Dean of the School of Justice, she was a member of the faculty at the University of Illinois, at the Hebrew University of Jerusalem, and the University of Chicago. She is currently university professor in the School of Public Affairs and the Washington College of Law at American University.

She has authored twenty-eight books and edited seventeen including *Adoption Across Borders* with Howard Altstein (2000), *In the Golden Land: A Century of Russian and Soviet Jewish Immigration* (1997), *The Ambivalent Welcome: Media Coverage of American Immigration* with Susan Alexander

(1993), and *New Lives: The Adjustments of Soviet Jewish Immigrants in the United States and Israel* (1985).

Simon is currently the editor of *Gender Issues*. She served, from 1978 to 1981, as editor of *The American Sociological Review* and, from 1983 to 1986, as editor of *Justice Quarterly*. In 1966 she received a Guggenheim Fellowship.